calling? How does my anxious

grow in gratitude? Why do

n I discern God's voi

M000208629

nat is the abund

? What does it mean to work for the L

erve through my pain? How does my spo

e? How does Jesus love me

How is forgiveness freedom? Am I re

my life? How can I discern God's voice!

vercome temptations? What is a wis

oved? What is my calling

What does it mean to work for the Lo

parent? Why do I need to serv

What is God's wi

erous people joyful?

How can I grow in gratitude?

to serve through my pain? What is my

at is God's will for my life? How c

How can I overcome temptations? How is forgiveness freedom?

How (

What is a wise financial plan? W

Why are generous people joyfu

es Jesus love me? Why do I need to

eness freedom? Am I ready to c

can I discern God's voice! How can I grow in gratitude

dom? What is God's will for

s a wise financial plan? How can I

ow does my spouse need to be

v can I discern God's voice! What is the abundant life

How to wisely

k for the Lord? Why are ge

an I discern God's voice!

To ....

From ....

Date ....

WISDOM
for *Living*

A 40-day Devotional for Practical,
Intentional, Wise Living

BOYD BAILEY

WISDOM FOR LIVING

Published by iDisciple Publishing, 2555 Northwinds Parkway, Alpharetta GA 30009.

ISBN: 978-1-7340486-1-2

Printed in China

WISDOM for *Living*

The Author
BOYD BAILEY

Meet the Author

BOYD BAILEY

*B*oyd began serving National Christian Foundation as President of the Georgia division in March, 2016. Prior to that time, Boyd was the co-founder and CEO of *Ministry Ventures*, a faith-based nonprofit, where he has trained and coached over 1,000 ministries in the best practices of prayer, board, ministry models, administration, and fundraising. Prior to Ministry Ventures, Boyd was the *National Director for Crown Financial Ministries* and an Associate Pastor at First Baptist Church of Atlanta. Boyd serves on numerous boards, including: Ministry Ventures, Wisdom Hunters, and Souly Business.

He is the author of Wisdom Hunters devotionals, and is the founder of Wisdom Hunters, Inc., an Atlanta-based ministry created to encourage Christians to apply God's unchanging truth in a changing world.

Boyd received his Bachelor of Arts from Jacksonville State University and his Masters of Divinity from Southwestern Seminary. Boyd and his wife, Rita, live in Roswell, Georgia. They have been married 40 years and are blessed with four daughters and four sons-in-law who love Jesus, and nine grandchildren. Boyd enjoys reading classical literature, business trends, theology, and digital news. He and Rita like to hike, travel, sit by the fire in the mountains, enjoy a cup of coffee at home, and walk on the beach. Missions, travel, and investing in young couples are passions as well. What is most enjoyable for Boyd is to get quiet before the Lord in prayer and Bible reading.

Introduction

Wise living is all about the Lord Jesus Christ. What is His best? What is His will? What are His ways when I'm puzzled about the wise thing to do? Sometimes I find myself inexperienced concerning the situation I face. I might lack confidence or objectivity in making the right judgment. Hallelujah, my heavenly Father wants me to know Him and know His plan for my life. My Lord longs for me to walk with Him in His ways.

Wise living requires keeping the realization and understanding of God at the center of our thinking. An awareness of Christ becomes the centerpiece to our core beliefs. *What would Jesus do?* Grows into a way of life. His desires, His motivations, His thoughts, and His character capture our imagination. This leads to wise living, for it is Christlike living.

"Who is wise? Let them realize these things. Who is discerning? Let them understand. The ways of the LORD are right; the righteous walk in them, but the rebellious stumble in them" (Hosea 14:9). Wisdom for living is a treasure from above that is found through humble seeking. It is found first in the person of Jesus Christ: "Christ the power of God and the wisdom of God" (1 Corinthians 1:24). To know Him is to know and understand godly wisdom. The life of Jesus illustrates wisdom for us, and His teaching educates us in wisdom. Indeed, it is in relationship with God the Son that Christians are able to grow in godly wisdom.

God the Father gives wisdom to those who ask in faith: "If any of you lacks wisdom, you should ask God, who gives generously to all without finding fault, and it will be given to you. But when you ask, you must believe and not doubt" (James 1:5-6). Trusting children of God have access to wisdom from their generous heavenly Father.

God the Spirit reveals wisdom to those who love Him: "These are the things [wisdom] God has revealed to us by his Spirit. The Spirit searches all things, even the deep things of God" (1 Corinthians 2:10). The Holy Spirit gives us discernment to know the difference between authentic wisdom from the Almighty and the counterfeit wisdom of the world.

God is gracious to give us wisdom through grace from God the Father—through relationship with God the Son—by revelation from God the Spirit.

"Who is wise and understanding among you? Let them show it by their good life, by deeds done in the humility that comes from wisdom" (James 3:13).

Wisdom is required more often than we realize. It is wisdom that cuts through emotion and gets to the reality of the situation. "What is the wise thing to do?" is an effective question in decision-making. "What is best for the enterprise?" is a wise question to ask as it relates to business and ministry.

Gaining true wisdom requires humility. This is what qualifies us to receive wisdom, because God knows a humble heart can be trusted with knowledge and understanding. Humility remembers that the origin of wisdom rests in Christ, the wisdom of God. And a humble person uses the influence of their wisdom for the good of others. It is at the feet of Jesus in prayer and dependence that our Lord fills our mind with His thoughts. "With humility comes wisdom" (Proverbs 11:2).

There is a worldly wisdom that competes with the wisdom of God. Every day I have to decide which world I will go to for knowledge and understanding. Will I humbly pursue the unseen resources of heaven, or will I proudly rely on the seen solutions offered on Earth? God's wisdom leads us to Christ, but the world's wisdom denies Him. The wisdom of God is unfathomable, but the world's wisdom is limited.

The question is, are you soliciting wisdom on a consistent basis? Knowledge and experience mixed with common sense and discernment is a great recipe for wisdom. Wisdom is seeking to understand God's perspective. This is why the wisdom found in God's Word is so relevant for living. The Bible is a treasure trove of wisdom waiting to be discovered by the discerning wisdom hunter. Seek out wisdom, and you will find something more valuable than money or possessions.

Don't merely pray, read, and meditate on the Bible, but also seek out wise people—those with gray hair who exhibit wise behavior. The wise will help you validate the inkling of wisdom you are beginning to grasp from your study of Scripture. Read books and listen to messages from men and women who are wise. Try to expose your mind and heart daily to sources of wisdom. Hang out long enough with wisdom, and it will rub off on you. So take every opportunity to call on wisdom. Be wise in your relationships. Be wise with your money. Be wise with your time. Your wisdom attracts others who are hungry for the same.

The Lord longs to shower His children with raindrops of wisdom.

He delights in imparting His game plan for living. However, it takes our daily pursuit for the wisdom of God to penetrate our thinking. Wise living defaults to a Biblical worldview of thinking. The ways of the Spirit are revealed as you understand and apply Scripture. This understanding of His personal concern for you invites you to have security and confidence in Him. Wise living is based on the character of God. "This calls for wisdom" (Revelation 13:18).

The Lord's wisdom is very practical for living an abundant life. It relates to building healthy relationships, managing money, making decisions, resolving conflict, growing a church or business, and planning for a family. Wisdom is God's perspective applied to common sense and proven principles that produce the best results.

Leaders don't need any more techniques, but they could use more godly wisdom. Parents don't need a one-size-fits-all approach to parenting, but they desperately need generous wisdom from their heavenly Father. Relationships under stress benefit from godly counsel, but more than anything—in humility—they need discernment and direction from the Holy Spirit. Wisdom applies at all times—with all people—in all cultures.

"The fear of the LORD is the beginning of knowledge, but fools despise wisdom and instruction" (Proverbs 1:7).

The crown jewel of wisdom accumulation is the fear of the Lord. The fear of God positions you to receive wisdom. No fear of God means no wisdom. No wonder our world is flush with fools! We have lost our fear of God, and thus wisdom has eluded us. The fear of the Lord is an incubator for wisdom. He gives wisdom to those who fear Him.

Love God, but fear Him. Worship God, but fear Him. Learn of God, but fear Him. Serve God, but fear Him. Your fear of God qualifies you for wisdom. Do not become so familiar with God that you lose your fear of God. This is unwise and leads to foolishness.

Wisdom awaits your harvest call. Pluck it and enjoy it, like plump, luscious, and juicy fruit on a hot summer day. Taste and see that wisdom is good. No one has ever complained of attaining too much wisdom. So call on wisdom often. Seek out the wise, and ask them and God for wisdom. This is the wise thing to do!

By God's grace, let's all be wisdom hunters for His glory. Like Solomon (1 Kings 3:9-14), instead of asking for more money, recognition, and control—let's ask for wisdom from above. How happy it makes our heavenly Father when we seek to know and understand His heart, so we can live out our lives from His viewpoint. "The fear of the Lord is the key to this treasure" (Isaiah 33:6).

If you call out for insight and cry aloud for understanding, and if you look for it as for silver and search for it as for hidden treasure, then you will understand the fear of the Lord and find the knowledge of God. For the Lord gives wisdom.—Proverbs 2:3-6

Seeking to Live Wisely,

Boyd Bailey

Table of Contents

Table of Contents

DAY 1

Exchanged Life

You were taught, with regard to your former way of life, to put off your old self, which is being corrupted by its deceitful desires; to be made new in the attitude of your minds; and to put on the new self, created to be like God in true righteousness and holiness.

—Ephesians 4:22-24

There is a great exchange that takes place when a person places their faith in Jesus Christ. Their old way of living is replaced with living for the Lord. Their old way of thinking is replaced with thinking on the truth of Jesus. Their old way of speaking is replaced with speech that is sprinkled with the grace of God. The old has passed, the new has come. The life of Christ becomes the life of the follower of Christ. No longer are we led down the dead-end road of unrighteousness, but we are set free to journey down the less traveled road of righteousness. We give up what we could not keep—our life on Earth, in exchange for what we can keep—eternal life in heaven. To a watching world it seems foolish to give up for God, but what we get from God—forgiveness, peace, and love—is true life. "Since, then, you have been raised with Christ, set your hearts on things above, where Christ is, seated at the right hand of God. Set your minds on things above, not on earthly things. For you died, and your life is now hidden with Christ in God. When Christ, who is your life, appears, then you also will appear with Him in glory" (Colossians 3:1-4).

Have you surrendered yourself to your Savior Jesus? Have you given over to Him trust in your own goodness and good deeds in exchange for His holiness and His Spirit-filled power? This great exchange of the temporal for the eternal is what gives you the capacity to grow in grace and to become a person of great faith. However, an effective exchange requires the receiver to have faith in the giver. God is a generous giver who can be trusted.

Make this great eternal exchange and do not waste another day. No one has ever regretted receiving from Almighty God His agenda for their life. The Lord wants you in exchange for Him. Jesus wants your life in exchange for His life. He wants your troubled heart in exchange for His tender heart. He wants your fears in exchange for His peace and calm.

> *No one has ever regretted receiving from Almighty God His agenda for their life.*

"If you declare with your mouth, 'Jesus is Lord,' and believe in your heart that God raised Him from the dead, you will be saved. For it is with your heart that you believe and are justified, and it is with your mouth that you profess your faith and are saved" (Romans 10:9-10).

QUESTION FOR THOUGHT AND PRAYER

Have I exchanged my old lost and selfish life for Christ's new life of love, forgiveness, and service to others? If not, why not now?

RELATED READINGS

JOHN 17:3; ROMANS 5:12-21; GALATIANS 2:20; 1 JOHN 5:13; 2 TIMOTHY 1:9-10

NOTES

Jesus wants your
life in exchange
for His life.

DAY 2

Abundant Life

The thief does not come except to steal, and to kill, and to destroy. I have come that they may have life, and that they may have it more abundantly.

—John 10:10, nkjv

What is quality of life for the Christian? How does Christ define quality living? He offers abundant life, but what does this look like for those who love the Lord? Abundant life begins by receiving the gift of God in the life of Christ. "And this is the testimony: God has given us eternal life, and this life is in his Son" (1 John 5:11). Quality of life begins with eternal life as the end goal. Abundant life is the reward for our salvation.

> *Quality of life means we live life motivated by what outcomes will live on into eternity.*

Quality of life means we live life motivated by what outcomes will live on into eternity. It will probably mean getting less and giving more in this life. By adjusting down my standard of living, I am able to give more toward what matters to Jesus. The Lord modeled well for us a life of quality. One example was His unselfish service: "In humility value others above yourselves, not looking to your own interests but each of you to the interests of others. In your relationships with one another, have the same mindset as Christ Jesus" (Philippians 2:3-5). Service to others brings quality of life to all parties.

Quality of life may not lead to ease and comfort, as our culture likes to advertise. Paul described his life of obedience to the Lord as a dangerous way, "I have been constantly on the move. I have been in danger from rivers, in danger from bandits, in danger from my fellow Jews, in danger from Gentiles; in danger in the city, in danger in the country, in danger at sea; and in danger from false believers" (2 Corinthians 11:26). You face danger, but knowing you live for Christ makes you persevere and trust Him.

How is your quality of life? Is it abundant in its obedience to Christ? Is He your life to the point where His priorities are your priorities? Do you let go of earthly indulgences so others can gain eternal rewards?

"I have been crucified with Christ. It is no longer I who live, but Christ who lives in me. And the life I now live in the flesh I live by faith in the Son of God, who loved me and gave himself for me" (Galatians 2:20, ESV).

QUESTION FOR THOUGHT AND PRAYER
Is my quality of life defined by Christ's
life at work in and through me?

RELATED READINGS
AMOS 6:1-7; ISAIAH 54:2; 2 PETER 1:3; REVELATION 2:7-10

NOTES

Quality of life on Earth
begins with eternal life
as the end goal.

DAY 3

Eternal Rewards

> *He regarded disgrace for the sake of Christ as of greater value than the treasures of Egypt, because he was looking ahead to his reward.*
>
> **—HEBREWS 11:26**

ternal rewards are based on a disciple's effort on Earth. Believers who ignore their spiritual opportunities and obligations will miss out on their heavenly Father's affirmation and remuneration. But those sober saints who take seriously their Savior's expectations will enter into the joy of their Master. Christ rewards obedience to Him.

Rewards in heaven are meant to be a godly motivation. Yes, our first response is to serve Jesus out of love and our overflowing gratitude for His goodness and grace. And it is wise to fear the Lord and allow our holy awe of the Almighty to be foundational for our life of faith and works. But there is an end in mind: Jesus wants His children to be devoted to and compelled by anticipating His generous gifts.

"For the Son of Man is going to come in his Father's glory with his angels, and then he will reward each person according to what they have done" (Matthew 16:27).

Renewing your mind with an eternal decision-making filter that facilitates biblical thinking and doing is a process. You can begin by asking the Lord in prayer how He wants you to invest your life in others. How does God want you to use your experience, your assets, your time, your money, and your influence for His purposes? In other words, how can you make eternal investments on Earth that bear fruit for God's glory?

What you do does not get you to heaven—that comes only by faith in Christ and God's amazing grace. But what you do after becoming a follower of Jesus does determine the quality of your eternal experience. The persecuted and martyred in this life have a great reward waiting in the next life. Those who initiate resources and influence on behalf of the poor and needy bring great satisfaction to Jesus that He expresses in bountiful blessings. Indeed, He rewards all those who diligently seek Him by faith.

Remain faithful to God's call and look forward to His reward.

"And without faith it is impossible to please God, because anyone who comes to him must believe that he exists and that he rewards those who earnestly seek him" (Hebrews 11:6).

Love God and your reward will be great. Be a faithful witness who plants or waters the gospel of Jesus Christ and you will be rewarded by living forever with eternally grateful souls. Send your money ahead to heaven by aggressively giving it away on Earth. Resist—even reject—rewards from the culture so you are positioned to receive Christ's rewards. Remain faithful to God's call and look forward to His reward.

[Jesus said,] "Look, I am coming soon! My reward is with me, and I will give to each person according to what they have done" (Revelation 22:12).

QUESTION FOR THOUGHT AND PRAYER
How can I live my life in a way that honors
the Lord and looks forward to His rewards?

RELATED READINGS
PSALM 58:11; ISAIAH 49:4; EPHESIANS 6:8; COLOSSIANS 3:24

NOTES

_____

_____

_____

_____

_____

Jesus wants His children
to be devoted and grateful
by anticipating His
generous gifts.

DAY 4

We Not Me

Now you are the body of Christ, and each one of you is a part of it.

—1 Corinthians 12:27

There is a larger context to life than just living for self. A self-focused life leads to chronic frustration and an inability to reach one's full potential. Its demanding demur marginalizes wise counsel and only attracts insecure individuals. However, those who pray for what's best for the whole, themselves become whole. Everyone is honored in an environment where individual contributions are valued. "We not me" is the vocabulary of those who honor each other.

Every disciple is stronger when they are connected to other Christ followers. Isolation contributes to spiritual impotence, whereas community gives spiritual life. Encouragement and accountability are exalted in relationships that serve what's best for the group. A leader who serves the team motivates other team members to serve well. A man who serves his family experiences a family that serves each other. "We" overcomes "me" through unselfish service.

"Each of you should use whatever gift you have received to serve others, as faithful stewards of God's grace in its various forms" (1 Peter 4:10).

Our spiritual birth engrafted us as a member of Christ's body. We cannot detach an appendage of the Lord's, any more than a member of our physical body can be disassociated from the other body parts. So we pray for those around us who know Christ, and we get to know each other. Oh, the joy of being known and knowing others who love Him! Life that is truly life is lived in the margins with those submitted to our Savior Jesus.

The sequence for successful thinking is Him, them, and then you.

Are you motivated first by "He," second by "we," and lastly by "me"? If so, you are set up for relational fulfillment. The sequence for successful thinking is Him, them, and then you. "Me" will try to squeeze in and monopolize relationships, cannibalize conversations, and hijack heaven's agenda. By God's grace, we must put to death the "me monster" and replace it with love for the Lord and people. "We not me" is the motto of mature Jesus followers.

"Let no debt remain outstanding, except the continuing debt to love one another, for whoever loves others has fulfilled the law" (Romans 13:8).

QUESTION FOR THOUGHT AND PRAYER
*Whose needs can I put ahead of mine
through my prayers and service?*

RELATED READINGS
ROMANS 12:10-16; 14:13; 15:7; 2 CORINTHIANS 13:11; GALATIANS 5:13

NOTES

_____

_____

_____

_____

_____

_____

_____

_____

_____

_____

By God's grace, put to death the "me monster" and replace it with love for the Lord and people.

DAY 5

Spiritual Living

Those who belong to Christ Jesus have crucified the flesh with its passions and desires. Since we live by the Spirit, let us keep in step with the Spirit.

—GALATIANS 5:24-25

The Holy Spirit fuels spiritual living. This is where freedom resides and where fruit bearing takes place. The flesh is pre-conversion to Christ living; it is reliance on self to attain earthly security. The Spirit is post-conversion to Christ living; it is reliance on God to attain earthly and eternal security. The priorities of Spirit and the flesh conflict, but the flesh has been put to death by faith and the Spirit has come alive. Spiritual living submits to Christ.

Our spiritual life thrives as we daily surrender our soul to Jesus. The way we became a Christian—by grace through faith—is the same way we continue as a Christian. Yes, the flesh tries to flaunt its old habits as teasers for us to not trust God. But we know better—it is better to not boast in the flesh, but to be humbled by the Spirit. When we walk in the Spirit, we are empowered to bear the fruit of the Spirit.

"So I say, walk by the Spirit, and you will not gratify the desires of the flesh. For the flesh desires what is contrary to the Spirit, and the Spirit what is contrary to the flesh. They are in conflict with each other, so that you are not to do whatever you want" (Galatians 5:16-17).

Our spiritual life thrives as we daily surrender our soul to Jesus.

The Spirit brings wisdom in the moments when we are considering actions that are unwise. The Spirit brings conviction when we begin to drift from our convictions. The Spirit brings comfort when we struggle with discomfort. The Spirit leads us into God's will when we are tempted to follow our own will. In short, the Holy Spirit is heaven's secret to spiritual living. When we walk by the Spirit, we are everything; if we ignore the Spirit, we are nothing.

Are you looking to love better, rejoice more, and be at peace? If so, allow the Spirit to grow love, joy, and peace in the soil of your soul. God is your Gardner, and His green thumb of grace always grows an abundance of fruit. Forbearance, kindness, goodness, faithfulness, gentleness, and self-control are all seeded by the Holy Spirit to produce lasting, luscious fruit in our soul. Fertilize with faith and then water with God's Word.

Invite the Holy Spirit to pull out any weeds of sin from your heart, and like a kudzu plant climbs, coils, and covers in a hot and humid climate, the fruit of the Spirit will cover your life in Christlike character. Your part is to have faith, and His part is to produce fruit in you. Your part is surrender, and His part is victory. Your part is prayer, and His part is answers. Your part is humility, and His part is a harvest of righteousness. Spiritual living lives by the Spirit's power.

"You, however, are not in the realm of the flesh but are in the realm of the Spirit, if indeed the Spirit of God lives in you. And if anyone does not have the Spirit of Christ, they do not belong to Christ" (Romans 8:9).

PRAYER
Heavenly Father, I surrender to Your Spirit's empowering me to spiritual living.

RELATED READINGS
ROMANS 8:3-5, 14; 2 CORINTHIANS 5:17; COLOSSIANS 2:11; 1 PETER 2:16

NOTES

_____

_____

_____

_____

_____

The way we became a Christian—by grace through faith—is the same way we continue to grow as a Christian.

DAY 6

Appointments with God

Sow righteousness for yourselves, reap the fruit of unfailing love, and break up your unplowed ground; for it is time to seek the LORD, until he comes and showers his righteousness on you.

—HOSEA 10:12

ppointments with God honor God. When you schedule time with Him daily, it shows He is your priority. Some people clamor to get on a celebrity's calendar, yet Christ is accessible 24/7. Indeed, Jesus, the most iconic person of all time, is available to engage any interested individual at any time. Almighty God has no handlers or gatekeepers—He is easily reachable by faith. So, why are we reluctant to schedule time with eternity? Are we really too busy to pray?

In life, we have appointments for activities that truly matter to us: haircuts, exercise, doctors, dentists, mechanics, job interviews, breakfasts, lunches, dinners, and dates. Why not schedule time with our Savior so we feel accountable to meet with Him? We would certainly not miss an appointment with Jesus any more than we would stand up our hairstylist. Putting an appointment on our calendar makes it easier to say, "I have another commitment."

"This is what the Lord says to Israel: 'Seek me and live'" (Amos 5:4).

We set appointments with the Lord because He is the ultimate expert for living. He is your relational therapist, He is the minister of your soul, He is the psychiatrist of your emotions and the physician of your body. God is your eternal expert for how to do life meaningfully and abundantly. Go to God to learn how to go forward in amazing faith-filled living. Your appointments with the Almighty teach you how to live life well.

What is keeping you from putting time with Christ on your calendar? Time? He has given you enough time to do His will. Fatigue? Rest in the arms of your heavenly Father. Faith? When you show up, He shows up and helps your unbelief. Feelings? Eventually, your emotions will catch up with your obedience to be with Jesus. God appointments work.

When you schedule time with Him daily, it shows He is your priority.

Perhaps you can start with scheduling five minutes a day with Christ, with a goal to increase it to an hour a day. Just as you turn off your phone and give full focus to those with whom you meet, do the same for your Savior. Give Him your undivided attention, with no multitasking or distractions. Create a calm place to be quiet before your Lord. Begin the day by feeding your soul, and then your fullness of faith will feed other starving souls.

"They were also to stand every morning to thank and praise the Lord. They were to do the same in the evening" (1 Chronicles 23:30).

PRAYER

Heavenly Father, my heart's desire is
to meet You at a daily appointed time.

RELATED READINGS

1 Samuel 1:19; Psalm 5:3; Zephaniah 2:3; Mark 1:35

NOTES

_____

_____

_____

_____

_____

_____

_____

_____

We set appointments with the Lord because He is the ultimate expert for living life to the fullest.

DAY 7

Urgent Prayers for Children

A Canaanite woman from that vicinity came to him, crying out, "Lord, Son of David, have mercy on me! My daughter is demon-possessed and suffering terribly." . . . [She] came and knelt before Him. "Lord, help me!" she said.

—Matthew 15:22, 25

Life circumstances can crush our faith or cause us to pray more earnestly. Especially when our children are in need, our resolve ratchets up more intensely. When we see our little one languishing in illness, we cry out to Christ for mercy. When our grown children reel from unwise decisions, our hearts break as we bring their needs before our Lord daily. Children caught in adversity require intense intercession.

Great trials require great faith; so prayerful parents kneel before their Savior Jesus and solicit mercy on behalf of their son or daughter. The pain of watching a child suffer is overwhelming for the mom or dad, and they need grace and mercy for their own emotional stability and peace of mind. Faithful parents both offer prayers and need the prayers of others.

But what happens when nothing happens? When Jesus is silent about your son's alternate lifestyle or drug abuse, do you stop soliciting heaven for help? When nothing changes with your daughter's promiscuity or pattern of lies, do you quit loving her? Of course

Children caught in adversity require intense intercession.

not. Grace does not give up, but doubles down in determination to plead with Christ for help and healing.

"Be joyful in hope, patient in affliction, faithful in prayer" (Romans 12:12).

Children or grandchildren caught in Satan's scheme of deception and irresponsible living need prayers flung to heaven with fervent entreaty. Jesus is listening. He cares. He can mend a broken heart and make it much better than before. The crumbs of mercy from Christ's table of trust feed hungry souls who never stop worshiping their Lord. So in your trial, or in your support of a loved one who is under severe affliction, stay true to pray and trust Jesus. Cry out to Christ for healing and relief. Receive His reassurance; resolve not to give up going to God for grace and mercy in your time of need. Great faith gets great results because we serve a great and compassionate God.

"Let us then approach the throne of grace with confidence, so that we may receive mercy and find grace to help us in our time of need" (Hebrews 4:16).

PRAYER

Heavenly Father, I cry out for children who desperately need Your healing touch and loving care. In Jesus' name, amen.

RELATED READINGS
ISAIAH 38:19; MATTHEW 19:13; LUKE 15:20; JOHN 11:4

NOTES

_____

_____

_____

_____

_____

_____

_____

_____

Resolve not to give up going to God for grace and mercy in your time of need.

DAY 8

Listen to the Lord's Voice

You do not believe because you are not my sheep. My sheep listen to my voice; I know them, and they follow me. I give them eternal life, and they shall never perish; no one will snatch them out of my hand.

—JOHN 10:26-28

I confess, sometimes as a husband I drift into selective listening when my wife says things that I don't want to hear or when my mind is preoccupied with a project or a problem. The consequences of my unwillingness or inability to listen well, or not at all, is at best being insensitive to my sweetheart and at worst being disrespectful and unloving.

When she calls me out of my fog, it is best to not lamely defend myself and say, "I was listening," but rather to confess my folly in checking out while in her presence and ask her forgiveness.

Listening requires attention! All types of voices compete for mindshare, but it's the voice of my Lord that deserves my undivided attention and discernment. Do I listen intently to His directives so I can avoid straying into the danger areas of temptation and disobedience? Am I seeking my approval

...it's the voice of my Lord that deserves my undivided attention and discernment.

from the One whose acceptance matters the most?

Jesus says that if I truly love Him, I will listen to Him, learn from Him, and follow Him wholeheartedly: "Whoever has my commands and keeps them is the one who loves me. The one who loves me will be loved by my Father, and I too will love them and show myself to them" (John 14:21).

Are you in tune with the Lord? What is He saying that might be countercultural, but is truly best for you and your family? The courage to say no or the faith to say yes requires the Holy Spirit's leadership and Christ's peace that surpasses all understanding.

Don't dismiss the example of other faithful followers in the flock of God. Look to those who have labored to listen, who know how to hear the voice of their sympathizing Shepherd, who feast with delight in the green pastures of His provision and rest by still waters, at peace and secure.

The Lord's voice becomes clearer in quietness. Get quiet, focus, and learn wisdom in the secret place of the soul, where only your Savior dwells. Your Father finds great pleasure in sharing His ways with the humble and upright of heart. Your integrity is an instrument of God's will—He uses it to bless you so you can bless others. Whatever success you experience, offer it to Jesus as a sacrifice of praise and thanksgiving. You are the most vulnerable to temptation when you are triumphant, so stay surrounded by those who will tell you the truth. Listen to their godly advice as you listen to the One who spoke in your mother's womb!

"She had a sister called Mary, who sat at the Lord's feet listening to what he said" (Luke 10:39).

PRAYER

Dear Lord, by faith I listen intently to You, the Great Shepherd of my soul. Give me ears to hear. In Jesus' name, amen.

RELATED READINGS

EXODUS 33:11; 1 SAMUEL 3:10; PROVERBS 19:20; ISAIAH 51:1; LUKE 8:8

NOTES

_____

_____

_____

_____

_____

If I truly love Jesus, I will listen to Him, learn from Him, and follow Him wholeheartedly.

Relational

WISDOM

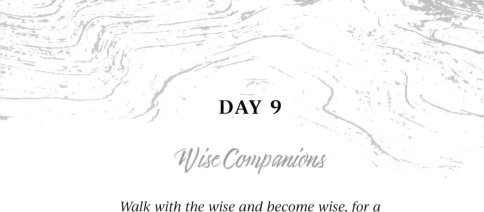

DAY 9

Wise Companions

Walk with the wise and become wise, for a companion of fools suffers harm.

—Proverbs 13:20

What is your definition of a quality life? Good health? Harmony at home? A happy heart? Financial security? Freedom of speech and worship? A fulfilling career? Grateful and contented children? A meaningful marriage? A life of significance? Peace with God? Probably some of these elements and more make up a life worth living—a quality life.

The quality of our life is determined by the quality of our relationships. Who we spend time with is who we become. If we spend time with those who are wise in their finances, and if we pay attention, we can become wise in our finances. If we are intentional in our faith, we will worship with those of great faith. Our life is a reflection of our relationships.

"Therefore I urge you to imitate me. For this reason I have sent to you Timothy, my son whom I love, who is faithful in the Lord. He will remind you of my way of life in Christ Jesus, which agrees with what I teach everywhere in every church" (1 Corinthians 4:16-17).

So, how is your relational portfolio? Are you diversified, with people who bring value to all aspects of your life? Conversely, are you intentional to invest time and interest in those who look to you for guidance? Quality of life flows from not just receiving wisdom, but from giving wisdom. Wisdom works both directions for the good of the relationship.

Furthermore, be careful not to excuse bad behavior because you are trying to relate to questionable company. Draw a line far away from eroding your character's credibility. You can influence others for good without being bad. In some situations, what you don't do defines you more than what you do. Use business trips and vacations to model faithfulness, not foolishness. Stand for what's right— even when others agree to what's wrong.

Our life is a reflection of our relationships.

"Do not be misled: 'Bad company corrupts good character'" (1 Corinthians 15:33).

Above all, quality of life results from your relationship with Christ. He is life itself, and everything good in life flows from Him. When you grow in your personal relationship with Jesus, it affects the growth of your other relationships. Relationship-building in heaven builds relationships on Earth. Ultimately, Jesus is the life to model and follow. The resurrected life of Christ gives you the spiritual stamina to experience a quality life.

"Jesus said to her, 'I am the resurrection and the life. The one who believes in me will live, even though they die; and whoever lives by believing in me will never die. Do you believe this?' 'Yes, Lord,' she replied, 'I believe . . .'" (John 11:25-27).

QUESTION FOR THOUGHT AND PRAYER

Who are the wise people I spend time with?
Am I investing in quality relationships?

RELATED READINGS
PSALM 56:13; 2 CORINTHIANS 6:14; PHILIPPIANS 2:1-4; 1 JOHN 1:7

NOTES

_____

_____

_____

_____

_____

_____

_____

The quality of our life is determined by the quality of our relationships.

DAY 10

Learn to Forgive

And be kind to one another, tenderhearted, forgiving one another, even as God in Christ forgave you.

—Ephesians 4:32, nkjv

*F*orgiven people forgive because they are eternally grateful for the grace of God's forgiveness in their hearts. They are keenly aware that outside of Christ, they are cursed to a cycle of unforgiveness—lost in their sins. They know that the Lord raised them up forgiven so they, in turn, can forgive. Forgiveness on Earth flows from forgiveness in heaven, and it is something to be passed on today, not to be stored away for some future occasion.

Unforgiveness encroaches on the health of our relationships. It is like a cancer that eats away at our enjoyment of God, family, and friends. Suddenly, without advance notice, we lash out at those we love—all because of someone we don't love. Unforgiveness, like an inactive but rumbling volcano, waits to explode at any moment of disappointment. The embroiled embers smolder like sin and will erupt when pressure shakes its foundation.

Do you hold a grudge that has a hold on you? Does resentment hang over you like a bad dream, only you never wake up? This level of emotional upheaval is no way to live for the Lord. His will is not for you to be preoccupied with people who have stolen your joy and hindered your fellowship with Jesus. Forgiveness frees you from the acrid taste of bitterness and replaces it with the sweet taste of grace. Therefore, forgive like you're forgiven.

True forgiveness is sincere and all-inclusive. We are not in a position to judge who deserves forgiveness and who does not. One test to determine if you are doing that is to ask if you are tenderhearted or hard-hearted toward others. A hard heart has yet to be broken by heaven's caring crush. It may take extended adversity to soften your heart to forgive.

Forgiveness on Earth flows from forgiveness in heaven.

Why wait in anxious resentment when you can be freed today from hatred and relational apathy? Make your forgiveness specific. Communicate clearly that you are forgiving an exact amount of money—they are no longer in debt to you. Did a relative abuse you as a child? Were you fired over office politics? Talk with them—if they have abandoned you or are dead, write a letter expressing Christ's love and your forgiveness.

What if you forgive someone and they are unresponsive and unrepentant? You cannot control another's response, only yours. Trust that the Lord is working in their hearts and that your humble and sincere example will begin a work of grace in their heart. Love and kindness tear down walls of anger; grace and forgiveness build bridges of hope. Satan's destructive deception is exposed and destroyed in the face of your forgiveness.

". . . What I have forgiven—if there was anything to forgive—I have forgiven in the sight of Christ for your sake, in order that Satan might not outwit us. For we are not unaware of his schemes" (2 Corinthians 2:10-11).

QUESTION FOR THOUGHT AND PRAYER

Who needs my total forgiveness? What is the best method for me to forgive them?

RELATED READINGS
MICAH 7:18; JEREMIAH 33:8; LUKE 7:47; HEBREWS 8:12

NOTES

_____

_____

_____

_____

_____

Forgiven people forgive because they are eternally grateful for the grace of God's forgiveness in their hearts.

DAY 11

Love Her

> *Under three things the earth trembles; under four it cannot bear up . . . an unloved woman when she gets a husband.*
>
> — **Proverbs 30:21, 23,** ESV

What does a woman long for from her husband? Simply love. A husband's love is like a fresh breath from heaven for a wife who feels vulnerable and at times fearful. His love is a rock of refuge after she reels from a relational conflict at work, at church, or from another family member. The love of her husband goes a long way in satisfying that deep desire of a woman to love and be loved.

"His banner over me is love" (Song of Solomon 2:4, NASB). Husbands, a gracious woman is not to be taken advantage of or to be taken for granted. Instead, thank God for a wife who wants to please the Lord and serve her family. When was the last time you loved your bride in a way that she wants you to love her; in a way that only you can love her? Have you asked her lately what would make her feel loved by you? Outside of Christ's love, your love is the most meaningful, valuable, and satisfying love to your spouse. She needs to know that all of you belongs to her and all of her belongs to you. There should never be a feeling of competition for your attention between your wife and another woman; dismiss this danger at the outset. Make your wife feel your fidelity—you are a one-woman man and have eyes for no other.

"My beloved is mine and I am his" (Song of Solomon 2:16).

How can you learn to love your wife? Ask her. Seek out men who love their wives well and gain insights from them. Ask God. He is the Lord of love and the Lord over your marriage. Go to the source of love, your Savior Jesus, and He will instruct you in the way you can love your wife unconditionally. By God's grace, love your wife by protecting her. Love her by trusting her. Love her by giving her encouragement and hope. And always love her through the good times and the bad times. Love her with your words, love her with your time, and love her with gifts and kind words. A wife loved well by her husband is beautiful to behold—she is a trophy of God's grace.

What does a woman long for from her husband? Simply love.

"It always protects, always trusts, always hopes, always perseveres" (1 Corinthians 13:7).

QUESTION FOR THOUGHT AND PRAYER

How does my wife want me to love her?
How does God want me to love my wife?

RELATED READINGS

ECCLESIASTES 9:9; HOSEA 3:1; 1 CORINTHIANS 13; EPHESIANS 5:25-26

NOTES

_____

_____

_____

_____

_____

_____

_____

_____

_____

_____

A wife loved well by her husband is beautiful to behold—she is a trophy of God's grace.

DAY 12

Respect Him

The wife must respect her husband.

—EPHESIANS 5:33

*I*n the same way a wife longs to be loved, a husband longs to be respected. Knowing that he can fulfill his role as provider and leader is a catalyst for his self-confidence. Most men question their ability to be everything they need to be for their family, but insecurities become insignificant in a home where a husband feels respect. A wife's support energizes her man like jet fuels a booster rocket.

Husbands need the support of their wives. It works both ways, of course, as the wife needs to feel the support of her husband, but this is even more crucial for a man. A God-fearing husband knows that the Lord has placed him in a position of leadership in his home. It is overwhelming sometimes, because of the pressures of life. The last thing a husband needs to feel is distance or distrust from his wife. Her spousal support may be the only thing that is preventing him from giving up.

"He must manage his own family well and see that his children obey him, and he must do so in a manner worthy of full respect" (1 Timothy 3:4).

Wives, do not underestimate the importance of your support for your husband. Your affirmation is a valuable and powerful catalyst for his ongoing success. Men are not as self-sufficient as they might seem. On the outside, we may seem invincible, but on the inside, we are needy and desperate for recognition and validation. A man needs to know his wife trusts his decision-making and his ability to provide for his family.

Your confidence in your husband propels his confidence in himself to higher levels.

Your confidence in your husband propels his confidence in himself to higher levels. Your belief in him builds him up to believe in himself. It is difficult for a man to rise any higher than the opinion of his helpmate. Men long to be built up by their brides. Brag on him in public and affirm him in private. Look to your husband as the leader God has placed in your life.

Pray for your husband to lead lovingly and wisely. Be patient, and don't usurp his authority when things are not getting done in your way or your timing. Trust God to work in his heart; God can handle him much better than your "creative consequences." View your husband in the light of eternity. God wants him to grow up and give spiritual leadership, so let him lead—even when it means he fails. Your respect can grow the heart of your husband to love well.

"Give to everyone what you owe them: If you owe taxes, pay taxes; if revenue, then revenue; if respect, then respect; if honor, then honor" (Romans 13:7).

QUESTION FOR THOUGHT AND PRAYER

How can I respect my husband in a way that encourages him and also honors the Lord?

RELATED READINGS

DEUTERONOMY 1:15; PROVERBS 31:23; LUKE 11:43; 1 TIMOTHY 3:2-4

NOTES

_____

_____

_____

_____

_____

_____

_____

_____

_____

_____

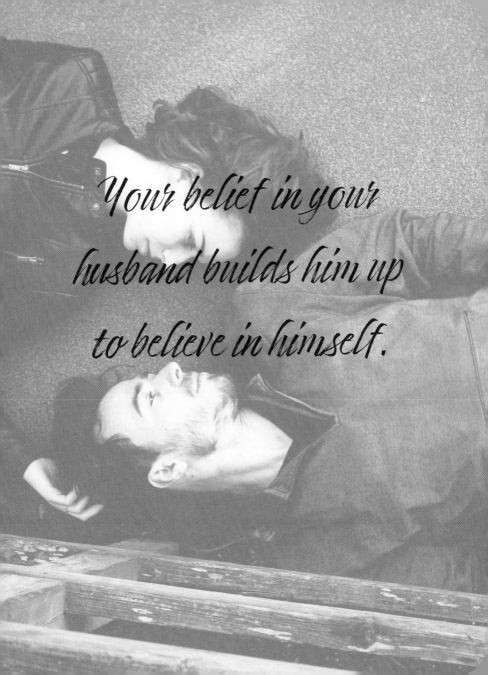

Your belief in your husband builds him up to believe in himself.

DAY 13

Model the Way

> *You became imitators of us and of the Lord,*
> *for you welcomed the message in the midst of*
> *severe suffering with the joy given by the Holy*
> *Spirit.*

> **—1 THESSALONIANS 1:6**

Parents are in a unique position to model right living to their children. The role of father and mother carries a humbling responsibility—to be a parent worth following. Whether they like it or not, parents are the Lord's authority over their little ones, and it's imperative they take seriously their obligation to steward well their parental roles.

What a privilege to present Christ to our progeny in our speech, actions, and attitude. Indeed, our words carry weight when our actions align with Almighty God's expectations. The Lord wants parents to depend on Him for wisdom and direction, and then to plant the same seeds of dependence on God in the hearts of their children at home. A parent who regularly prays for Christ's provision will inspire their son or daughter to do the same.

"Listen, my sons, to a father's instruction; pay attention and gain understanding" (Proverbs 4:1).

A child is most motivated to walk wisely when their loving parents live it out before them. A child who sees their parents persevering in prayer will learn the discipline of longsuffering. A child or teenager who observes their father and mother serving the poor, caring for aging parents, and giving generously to God's work wants to do the same. The best way for a young boy or girl to learn is to serve alongside their parents.

What a privilege to present Christ to our progeny in our speech, actions, and attitude.

Jesus is not looking for perfect parents, but for fathers and mothers who will live by faith and not by sight. The Lord longs for parents whose public profession of faith matches their private conduct and character. Your child may or may not remember what you say, but there is a high probability that they will become who you are.

Therefore, seek the Lord together first as husband and wife— and then as a family. God will give you the grace to model for your children a life of love and forgiveness. Pray with them and for them to walk in the truth, while trusting in the Lord. Do not underestimate the power of your influence on your little ones. You are God's representative of righteousness to their tender hearts; be a compelling example for Christ.

"Children's children are a crown to the aged, and parents are the pride of their children" (Proverbs 17:6).

QUESTION FOR THOUGHT AND PRAYER

How can we be an example to our children that causes them to love Christ?

RELATED READINGS

ISAIAH 38:19; JEREMIAH 32:18; MALACHI 4:6; LUKE 2:27

NOTES

_____

_____

_____

_____

_____

_____

_____

_____

A child is most motivated to walk wisely when their loving parents live it out before them.

DAY 14

Teach and Train

Pains as of a woman in childbirth come to him, but he is a child without wisdom; when the time arrives, he doesn't have the sense to come out of the womb.

—Hosea 13:13

*C*hildren need to be taught wisdom. A wise parent's goal is to grow a wise child. After all, wise children become wise adults. Yes, sometimes it's hard for them to grasp wisdom because of their age and stage in life, but the effort to impart wisdom is worth your while. Indeed, wisdom—the ability to understand and apply God's Word to life—is one of the most wonderful gifts you can give your child.

Make wisdom inviting and practical so that your children can expand their perspective and make wise decisions. Stories stir the heart and illuminate the mind. Use this to your advantage in teaching your children. Tell stories of individuals who made wise decisions and the positive effects that followed. Then contrast these uplifting illustrations with stories about people who chose an unwise path and suffered harm as a result. We owe it to our offspring to engage them in conversations about real-life people. Otherwise, they stay oblivious in a bubble of unrealistic living.

Allow your children to spread their wings and begin decision-making while they still live under your roof. Start them out young by helping them make money decisions. Show them the pattern of "share, save, and spend" from your own financial management. Then lead them to do the same. Watch them smile as they experience the joy of generosity. Be proud as their discipline and patience grows when they are able to save for something they want. Be an example of smart spending, and you may become a recipient of its fruit as your child learns how to be a savvy shopper. Financial wisdom is a practical gift you can give to your child.

Good judgment in choosing friends is another facet of teaching your child the ways of wisdom. Wisdom does not settle for the shallow acceptance of just any friend. Make sure your children understand the propensity to be like the people they "hang out with" (Proverbs 13:20). It is wise to choose friends whose faith is growing and robust. Encourage friendships that lift up, instead of those who pull down. Teach them that it is unwise to flirt with friendships that dilute growth with God. Discuss with your children why they need to avoid friendships that drive a wedge between child and parent. Challenge your children to pray for friends who complement their faith and move them closer to their heavenly Father. Wise friends rub off on your children in wise ways.

> *You can be at peace when you have a child who is wise in the ways of God.*

Lastly, discuss with your children regularly the wisdom of God (Proverbs 2:6). Read the Bible with them and discuss the meanings of particular verses. Make the discussion of Scripture a part of your everyday life. Take your Bible to church. Underline the phrases that leap from the page into your heart and mind. Discuss its application to your life over lunch. Ask your child to hold you accountable to the truth God is teaching you.

God's wisdom will follow your children for the rest of their lives. It will be with them when you are absent. You can be at peace when you have a child who is wise in the ways of God.

QUESTION FOR THOUGHT AND PRAYER
What are you doing to help your children become wise?

RELATED READINGS
PROVERBS 22:6; LUKE 2:52; EPHESIANS 6:4; 2 TIMOTHY 3:15

NOTES

Wisdom comes by allowing children to spread their wings and begin their own decision-making while they still live under your roof and protection. Rela-

DAY 15

Relational Generosity

Therefore I [Paul] am all the more eager to send him [Epaphroditus], so that when you see him again you may be glad and I may have less anxiety. So then, welcome him in the Lord with great joy, and honor people like him, because he almost died for the work of Christ.

—PHILIPPIANS 2:28-30

Relational generosity—introducing two people to one another for their mutual benefit—is the richest form of giving. My willingness to use my influence to bring together two people for the sake of a growing relationship can become a fruitful investment for all of us. I am a much richer person today because friends have unselfishly introduced me to their friends over the years. Many times I gained a new friend who became a messenger of Christ for me in that season of my life. Relational generosity is a catalyst for God's will because Jesus works through people.

Paul was open-handed with his loyal friend Epaphroditus. His love for his brother, coworker, and fellow soldier in the faith did not keep Paul from sharing this stellar servant of the Lord with other needy saints. Though Paul was suffering in a Roman prison, he willingly commissioned his trusted friend to serve other friends at a church hundreds of miles away in Philippi. And he implored those benefiting from Epaphroditus' sacrifice to joyfully welcome him in the Lord. Grateful recipients of relational generosity honor both the gift and the giver.

"For he [Epaphroditus] longs for all of you [Philippi church] and is distressed because you heard he was ill. Indeed he was ill, and almost died. But God had mercy on him, and not on him only but also on me [Paul], to spare me sorrow upon sorrow" (Philippians 2:26-27).

What friend or acquaintance needs an introduction to someone you know?

What friend or acquaintance needs an introduction to someone you know? Someone suffering from an emotional or physical illness may need an introduction to a doctor you know who specializes in their area of pain. A new friend out of work could use your recommendation to a company you know is hiring. Maybe you need to release a friend for a season so they can serve the Lord in another part of the world. Relational generosity is risky. Things may not work out or someone may get hurt. But its potential benefits are worth the risk. Your part is to obey and patiently trust God to work out His will.

"I [Paul] have received full payment and have more than enough. I am amply supplied, now that I have received from

Epaphroditus the gifts you [Philippian church] sent. They are a fragrant offering, an acceptable sacrifice, pleasing to God" (Philippians 4:18).

PRAYER

Heavenly Father, use me to introduce people who together can go further faster with You.

RELATED READINGS

MATTHEW 5:47; PHILIPPIANS 4:3; PHILEMON 1:2; 1 CORINTHIANS 16:18

NOTES

---

*tional generosity
is a catalyst for God's
will. Jesus works
through people.*

DAY 16

Relational Investments

> *Remember this: Whoever sows sparingly will also reap sparingly, and whoever sows generously will also reap generously.*
>
> **—2 Corinthians 9:6**

*W*ise individuals do not spend all their income. They develop a process of first giving and saving before they spend all their cash on themselves. The same principle applies to relationships; we can spend all our efforts seeking what others can do for us, or we can intentionally invest in their lives in ways that make them feel valued and appreciated. Investing in others brings them joy and provides the relational investor with dividends of delight: encouragement, hope, and reliable resources.

Paul describes the principle of sowing and reaping, and although he applies this analogy to generosity with money, the same can be said about relationships. An agrarian culture understood that well-prepared soil, sown with abundant quality seed, then cultivated and nurtured in conducive weather conditions, produces an abundant harvest. Generous reaping is the outcome of generous sowing. Likewise, when love, patience, kindness, and generosity are sown into a relationship, there is a reciprocal harvest in abundant fruit of the Spirit.

"Let us not become weary in doing good, for at the proper time we will reap a harvest if we do not give up" (Galatians 6:9).

What if you approached relationships wondering how you can give and not what you can get?

What if you approached relationships wondering how you can give and not what you can get? Seek out someone who may be younger, but is hungry to grow as a person and follow hard after God's heart. Schedule a monthly meeting to discuss their felt needs. Bring to the discussion ideas you have related to wise money management, an effective prayer life, and how to work with difficult people, to name a few. After your time, enjoy a meal together to deepen the relationship.

Relational investment for others flows out of your relational investment with your heavenly Father. Prayer sown in humility reaps a heart of faith. Bible reading sown in surrender reaps a heart of obedience. Praise and worship sown in gratitude reaps a heart of hope.

Dollar-cost average time with Christ and over time your *compounding interest* in others will grow exponentially and your intimacy with the Almighty will grow a ten-fold *return on investment* (ROI). Relational investments are your greatest asset, so continue to prosper in true riches.

"In this way they will lay up treasure for themselves as a firm foundation for the coming age, so that they may take hold of the life that is truly life" (1 Timothy 6:19).

PRAYER

Heavenly Father, keep me focused on investing time and resources with You and others so my relational investments bring honor and glory to You. In Jesus' name, amen.

RELATED READINGS

PROVERBS 11:25; MATTHEW 6:20; LUKE 16:11;
ROMANS 12:8, 13; 1 TIMOTHY 5:10

NOTES

_____

_____

_____

_____

_____

_____

When love, patience, kindness, and generosity are sown into a relation—ship, there is a reciprocal harvest in abundant fruit of the Spirit.

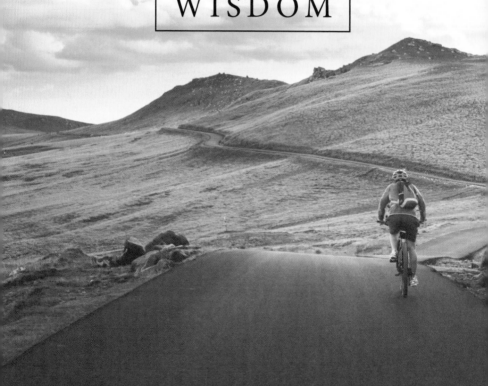

Physical

WISDOM

DAY 17

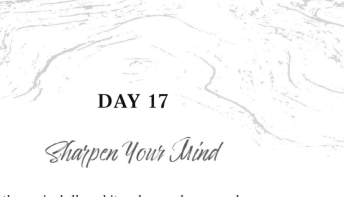

Sharpen Your Mind

If the ax is dull and its edge unsharpened, more
strength is needed, but skill will bring success.

—ECCLESIASTES **10:10**

Life is not meant to be full of endless activity and busyness. Without pauses, it loses its edge. A life worth living is one that takes the time to sharpen its skills. Skill-sharpening is an investment that will serve you well the rest of your life. Do not settle for mediocrity; by God's grace seek to be the best in your life roles. Your commitment to sharpen yourself is much like that of a farmer. A wise farmer will use his seasonal downtime to upgrade, replace, and repair his equipment. He sharpens the tips of his plow, rebuilds the tractor engines, and upgrades and cleans his equipment.

In the same spirit, there is a time to execute, and a time to regroup and sharpen yourself for the next initiative. He wants to use you to your full potential. Your part is to continually improve. Your activities and work will produce more lasting results when you take the time to hone heaven's gifts.

A skilled concert pianist practices the piano. A skilled writer searches out new words and becomes engrossed in sentence structures. A skilled speaker learns how to understand his audience and communicate one point in a variety of ways. A skilled mom quizzes other moms to gather mothering tips. A skilled golfer keeps practicing after the tournaments end; he hits balls into the night. Seek out new ways to keep your mind sharp and engaged in new ideas.

Your sharpened skills are an effective tool in the hand of God.

Your sharpened skills are an effective tool in the hand of God. Read about and learn from wise leaders of the faith whose writings have stood the test of time. Books are tremendous skill-sharpeners. Join a book club to ramp up your commitment and accountability. You can attend seminars or pursue a graduate degree. Use a variety of tools to stay sharp. Sparks fly when steel is sharpened, which means there will be some discomfort and growing pains. You are either moving forward or shrinking backward; there is no standing still. As you sharpen your skills, you are moving forward. You are stewarding God's talents and gifts to their fullest.

Swinging at issues with a dull life will lead you to the brink of giving up. Sharpen your mind with the Word of God. Nothing sharpens a mind like wisdom from above. God's principles are like a whetstone rock on a battered blade. He smoothes the jagged edges of your roughed-up life. Like an axe that has become chipped and blunted over time, your life can be refurbished by

God until it regains its radiant and shiny silver edge. Discover your skills through self-assessments and the counsel of others.

"Do you see a man skilled in his work? He will serve before kings; he will not serve before obscure men" (Proverbs 22:29).

PRAYER

Heavenly Father, I want to love You with my mind; keep me always a learner.

RELATED READINGS

EXODUS 31:6; PSALM 78:72; ACTS 17:29; 1 CORINTHIANS 14:37

NOTES

_____

_____

_____

_____

_____

_____

Sharpen your mind with the Word of God—nothing sharpens a mind like wisdom from above.

DAY 18

Eat Responsibly

When you sit to dine with a ruler, note well what is before you, and put a knife to your throat if you are given to gluttony. Do not crave his delicacies, for that food is deceptive.

—Proverbs 23:1-3

Responsible eating is a good indicator of responsible living. When we show discipline at the dinner table, we tend to exercise discipline in other areas of life as well. It's when we drift into indulging our appetite that we harm our bodies. Responsible eating means enjoying a delicious meal without gorging ourselves into gluttony. In general, portions pleasing to the palate need to decrease as our age increases.

Convenient access to good food can lead to cravings that spin out of control. Abundant and delicious meals make us overweight unless we moderate our intake and exercise our bodies. It is entertaining and relationally fulfilling to enjoy a nice meal with friends and family, but wisdom encourages temperance and moderation. An undisciplined appetite is destructive and unacceptable to the Lord.

"Their destiny is destruction, their god is their stomach, and their glory is in their shame. Their mind is on earthly things" (Philippians 3:19).

How can we, in good conscience, eat to excess when most of the world goes to bed hungry? Stewardship of food intake protects our body from excessive weight and invites undernourished bodies to gain weight. How much we eat and what we eat matters to our health and to the health of others. In our oblivious routine, we must not waste food while others waste away; we should eat less so others can eat more.

An undisciplined appetite is destructive and unacceptable to the Lord.

Eating is a spiritual transaction, as the fruit of the Spirit is self-control (Galatians 5:23). Therefore, enjoy the blessing of delicious meals with responsible eating. Dine with an eye on healthy food in smaller portions. Plan menus so you eat food with forethought and can avoid eating fast food too often. Your body will thank you for making food your friend rather than your enemy. Responsible eating honors the Lord by honoring His earthly temple.

"Don't you know that you yourselves are God's temple and that God's Spirit dwells in your midst? If anyone destroys God's temple, God will destroy that person; for God's temple is sacred, and you together are that temple" (1 Corinthians 3:16-17).

QUESTION FOR THOUGHT AND PRAYER
Do I eat responsibly? Am I careful to limit my cravings for food?

RELATED READINGS
DEUTERONOMY 21:20; PROVERBS 25:16; 1 CORINTHIANS 9:25-27; 2 PETER 1:6

NOTES

Responsible eating honors the Lord by honoring His earthly temple.

DAY 19

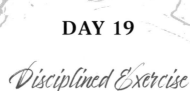

Disciplined Exercise

*I discipline my body like an athlete, training it to
do what it should.*

—1 CORINTHIANS 9:27, NLT

For the most part, Jesus walked everywhere he went; He had built-in exercise in His daily routine. These days, the comforts of society are actually in conflict with creating an exercise regimen. Discretionary time is filled with less important activities, to the detriment of keeping our bodies in a condition to be a blessing and not a burden.

For example, when we stay up late to watch television, we typically sleep later the next day. If morning is the best time to walk, run, lift weights, or engage in aerobics, then the probability of exercise is much lower. A disciplined life understands the need to schedule activities that complement one another. Disciplined exercise plans ahead.

"For the Spirit God gave us does not make us timid, but gives us power, love and self-discipline" (2 Timothy 1:7).

Yes, some followers of Jesus are more disciplined than others, but His Spirit empowers all who ask for self-discipline. A disciple of Jesus, by nature, leans into the Lord, motivated by discipline and determination. A disciple without discipline is like a mother without compassion—it is unnatural. We should see exercise as a stewardship of God's gift of health. Train your body to obey and serve the will of God for your life.

Point people to Jesus as you prepare His earthly temple for a life of love and worship.

"Do you not know that in a race all the runners run, but only one gets the prize? Run in such a way as to get the prize. Everyone who competes in the games goes into strict training. They do it to get a crown that will not last, but we do it to get a crown that will last forever" (1 Corinthians 9:24-25).

Some turn exercise into an idol and miss the point of good health as an offering to Jesus Christ. It is not for vainglory that we get into shape; rather, it is for the glory of God. We invest an hour a day in physical training so we can most effectively balance the day at work, home, and leisure. It is better to pay a trainer or gym a modest fee now than to wake up in the hospital one day with a catastrophic bill.

How does your fitness reflect your service for God? Do you take it for granted, or do you see it as a gift from the Lord to be managed well? Your health—good or bad—is a platform to proclaim the faithfulness of God. Do not use it to seek attention, but so others know you are a good steward of God's holy temple. Exercise for eternal purposes. Point people to Jesus as you prepare His earthly temple for a life of love and worship.

"No discipline seems pleasant at the time, but painful. Later on, however, it produces a harvest of righteousness and peace for those who have been trained by it" (Hebrews 12:11).

QUESTION FOR THOUGHT AND PRAYER

How can I create a routine in my life that incorporates disciplined exercise for God's glory?

RELATED READINGS

DANIEL 1:5; PROVERBS 5:23; 1 TIMOTHY 4:8; TITUS 1:8

NOTES

See exercise as a stewardship of God's gift of health and train your body to obey and serve the will of God for your life.

DAY 20

Humbled by Health

Naaman's servants went to him and said, "My father, if the prophet had told you to do some great thing, would you not have done it? How much more, then, when he tells you, 'Wash and be cleansed'!" So he went down and dipped himself in the Jordan seven times, as the man of God had told him, and his flesh was restored and became clean like that of a young boy.

—2 KINGS 5:13-14

When sickness seizes the body of a Christian, they are softened. There is a new sensitivity and tenderness of heart that may have been dormant before. They may have previously been a controlling Christian, but a body under fire from illness forces them to let go of control and cling to Christ. At first there may be an angry reaction, then there is a succumbing to a sense that God's got it—He is in control. Faith in the face of fiery trials is the fruit of humility. Sickness is an invitation to submit to Jesus.

As we walk in humility, we listen for the Lord's voice. He speaks through His Word, His teachers, His preachers, His children, and experts in treating physical ailments. Prayer and modern medicine are a powerful partnership in producing positive outcomes. A humbled heart creates clarity of mind for wisdom in decision-making. Humility invites healing.

"Jesus reached out his hand and touched the man. 'I am willing,' he said. 'Be clean!' And immediately the leprosy left him. Then Jesus ordered him, 'Don't tell anyone, but go, show yourself to the priest and offer the sacrifices that Moses commanded for your cleansing, as a testimony to them.' Yet the news about him spread all the more, so that crowds of people came to hear him and to be healed of their sicknesses" (Luke 5:13-15).

Humility invites healing.

Your cure may very well be different from another suffering saint's. It is a mystery why one body responds well to certain treatments while someone in a similar condition experiences a totally different result. So pray, do your research, and trust the Spirit to lead you in the Lord's physical plan for you. Don't miss the holistic approach of healing in your body, mind, will, emotions, and spirit. Humility is the gateway to God's grace and wholeness.

Allow the Lord to use health issues to bring vulnerability and intimacy into your relationships. Be real about your fears and feelings. Allow friends to comfort you. Emotional awareness and engagement is a healthy outcome of a humbled heart.

Renew your mind daily with the truth of Scripture and bend your will toward your biblical beliefs. Physical health is good, but spiritual wholeness is best. A humbled heart hears the Lord.

"Lord, do not forsake me; do not be far from me, my God. Come quickly to help me, my Lord and my Savior" (Psalm 38:21-22).

PRAYER
Heavenly Father, I humble my heart
so I can hear from You and be healed.

RELATED READINGS
JOB 14:22; PSALM 38:6-8; PROVERBS 17:22; MARK 7:37; 3 JOHN 1:2

NOTES

_____

_____

_____

_____

_____

Faith in the face of fiery trials is the fruit of humility. Sickness is an invitation to submit to Jesus.

DAY 21

Preemptive Physical Care

> *Daniel then said to the guard . . . "Please test your servants for ten days: Give us nothing but vegetables to eat and water to drink. . . ." At the end of the ten days they looked healthier and better nourished than any of the young men who ate the royal food.*

> — DANIEL 1:11-12, 15

*E*very soul saved by Jesus Christ is responsible to steward his or her body. In the same way the spirit of a person is cared for, so also their body needs proper attention. As age increases, a platform of physical care provides spiritual opportunities. Yes, some people are called to physically suffer for Christ's sake, but the Lord does not want His children to neglect their health. Bodies need intentional care.

The human body is a finely tuned complexity of cells, tissue, and organs, with Almighty God as the architect. Divine DNA determines the genes, but individuals write their medical history. This is why prayer and modern medicine are a responsible combination. We educate ourselves in what our bodies need to function best in a fallen world. We look to medical experts, learn from them, and ask the Lord for the wisest treatment for us.

"For you created my inmost being; you knit me together in my mother's womb. I praise you because I am fearfully and wonderfully made; your works are wonderful, I know that full well" (Psalm 139:13-14).

Prayerfully find a doctor you can trust and confide your fears in. View an internist as your friend and partner in healthy living. Do not be afraid of physical facts that require you to begin healthy habits; it's better to accept the truth of current health issues than to later discover an ounce of prevention could have saved a pound of cure.

Like Daniel, be different from the crowd and surround yourself with friends who have the conviction to eat right and exercise. Eating and drinking to the extreme limits your influence for the Lord. But a disciplined lifestyle leans into a routine of allowing past your lips only groceries untainted from man's toxic preservatives. Your body stays fresh when it is nourished by fresh foods. Slow down, plan healthy meals, and see how much better you feel.

...learn to see your health as an aspect of stewardship.

You are wise not to wait for disease to attack before you change. It is easier to take preventive measures now, before it's too late. So, schedule your annual physical, write out your menu for the week, increase your grocery budget, eat out less, and learn to see your health as an aspect of stewardship. Jesus expects you to love Him with your body and soul!

"And thou shalt love the Lord thy God with all thy heart, and with all thy soul, and with all thy mind, and with all thy strength: this is the first commandment" (Mark 12:30, KJV).

PRAYER

Lord, how would You have me take care of the body You have given me for Your glory?

RELATED READINGS

DEUTERONOMY 8:16; LEVITICUS 25:7; GALATIANS 2:20; EPHESIANS 5:29

NOTES

_____

_____

_____

_____

_____

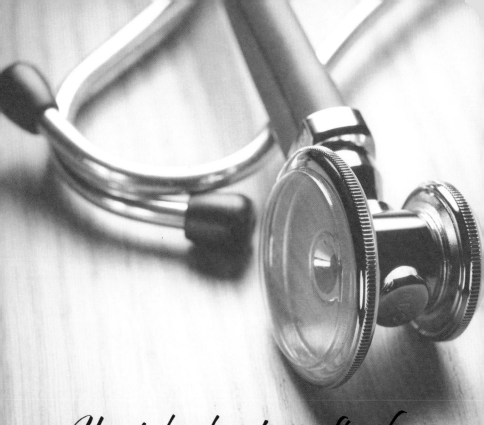

Your body stays fresh and energized when it is nourished by fresh foods.

DAY 22

Shadow of Death

Even though I walk through the darkest valley,
I will fear no evil, for you are with me; your rod
and your staff, they comfort me.

— **Psalm 23:4**

Everyone walks through life in the long shadow of death. There is no part of the globe where it can be avoided and no physical condition that can help us escape it. Death constantly knocks on the door of all demographics, all cultures, and all classes of people. We try to delay death's effects with surgery, medicine, diet, and exercise, but all of us eventually die.

Death for the dying can be a shadow of discomfort, discouragement, and even despair. It is in death's valley that faith is tested, families are stressed, and friends rally in prayer. How can you serve someone who is in their last months or days on Earth? First you live before them a life of faith. A dying loved one needs love from those who know the Lord, so that they can come to know the Lord. Those living in a valley need care, comfort, and heaven's hope.

Like Saul and Jonathan, allow death to bring you together as a family: "Saul and Jonathan—in life they were loved and admired, and in death they were not parted" (2 Samuel 1:23). Death is God's reminder that we need Him and we need each other.

We all walk toward death, but in Christ it is a passage to eternal life. It's hard when a believing parent begins to lose their ability to think clearly, but we can patiently listen to their irrational words, knowing one day they will speak with tongues of angels. It's even harder when an unbelieving parent begins to lose their faculties, because we wonder if they truly know Jesus. So we pray and trust that the reality of death brings them to the Lord.

> *We all walk toward death, but in Christ it is a passage to eternal life.*

"'Where, O death, is your victory? Where, O death, is your sting?' The sting of death is sin, and the power of sin is the law. But thanks be to God! He gives us the victory through our Lord Jesus Christ" (1 Corinthians 15:55-57).

Our faith in Jesus triumphs over death, and it also comforts us on the way to death. The destination of this life is death, but when we travel with the Lord, there is no need to fear evil or the unknown. His presence is all we need to persevere in righteous living. Hope, peace, and love are an outflow of walking with Jesus through the lonely valley of death.

Because of the passion of Christ, death's shadow is a passage through to paradise. The cross is a comfort to the dying and a bridge to heaven for those who believe in Jesus' death for their sin, His resurrection for their abundant life on Earth, and their eternal life in heaven. Jesus assured His disciples at His death, "Now is your time of grief, but I will see you again and you will rejoice, and no one will take away your joy" (John 16:22).

QUESTION FOR THOUGHT AND PRAYER
Am I walking with Jesus in my valleys?
Whom can I walk with through their valley?

RELATED READINGS
PSALM 56:13; PROVERBS 14:27; ISAIAH 38:10; JOHN 5:24; ROMANS 8:38

NOTES

_____

_____

_____

_____

_____

Those living in a valley need care, comfort, and heaven's hope.

DAY 23

Healthy Emotions Energize the Body

Love the Lord your God with all your heart.

—Mark 12:30

*P*eople who are emotionally healthy understand their flaws and accept their imperfections as evidence of their need for God's grace and forgiveness. Because they embrace this powerful truth, they are able to extend the same grace and forgiveness they have received from God to other people.

Emotionally healthy individuals take captive their thoughts, understand their feelings, and control their behavior. When facing life's challenges, they become better not bitter. They learn to process pain so it does not fester into ongoing relational conflict. Emotionally healthy people love God and are loved by God, so they are able to love for God. As a result, they experience peaceful relationships.

Jesus starts at the heart of the matter—our heart. Our heart is the seat of our feelings and affections. We are drawn to what we desire—what we value. Yes, the heart follows what it treasures above all else. In the same way an engaged person pursues the heart of their lover, so as the bride of Christ we passionately pursue His heart. As our heart loves Jesus, He simultaneously settles and stirs our emotions.

"A good man brings good things out of the good stored up in his heart, and an evil man brings evil things out of the evil stored up in his heart. For the mouth speaks what the heart is full of" (Luke 6:45).

If we serve in our own strength, we can quickly lapse into a loveless routine devoid of the Spirit's inner strength and power. Our emotions become frazzled and unruly without the riches of God's grace abundantly fueling our faith and love. Conversely, we grow our capacity to serve by being emotionally healthy—a healthy heart is able to encourage the hearts of others.

...a healthy heart is able to encourage the hearts of others.

Love is the most powerful weapon in our arsenal of faith—that's why Jesus starts with the heart in His sequence of how we can love God. Like the tip of an arrow, love points us to God. It commandeers all other graces to engage the Lord's affection and follow after His eternal concerns. When Jesus defined love as the greatest command, He gave us a glimpse into what He wants for the world and His children. A life motivated by love is only limited by its capacity to love the Lord and be loved by the Lord. Love is a muscle we exercise, so it grows in stamina and strength as we use it.

"Trust in him at all times, you people; pour out your hearts to him, for God is our refuge" (Psalm 62:8).

PRAYER

Heavenly Father, I submit to Your Spirit to be the manager and filter of my emotions. In Jesus' name, amen.

RELATED READINGS

2 KINGS 10:31; PROVERBS 10:11; JOHN 20:22; ACTS 2:33; REVELATION 22:17

NOTES

_____

_____

_____

_____

_____

_____

_____

_____

Emotionally healthy individuals take captive their thoughts, understand their feelings, and control their behavior.

DAY 24

Physical Care Plan

*Do you not know that your bodies are temples
of the Holy Spirit, who is in you, whom you have
received from God? You are not your own.*

—1 Corinthians **6:19**

*T*he Holy Spirit has such a high regard for our bodies that He makes His residence within us. Our body, His temple, is His holy habitation. Just as we wouldn't desecrate a church with unholy influences, so also we should not mistreat the temple of the Holy Spirit with unhealthy influences. Indeed, it is our spiritual responsibility to nourish and care for what God owns and allows us to inhabit. We should seek to make wise decisions in our physical care plan since our soul mate, God's Spirit, lives within us.

A plan to care for our body protects us from abuse and neglect. Yes, God's pinnacle of creation is fearfully and wonderfully made, as evidenced by its resilience to restore and heal itself. The Maker of our marvelous self expects us to love our body as He does. We care for ourselves so we can care for others.

"Husbands ought to love their wives as their own bodies. He who loves his wife loves himself. After all, no one ever hated their own body, but they feed and care for their body, just as Christ does the church" (Ephesians 5:28-29).

What does it mean for us to feed and care for our body as Christ does the church? Look at how He cherishes and nourishes the church, His body, with what is necessary for its growth, holiness, and happiness. In the same way, we should love our body by submitting it to a healthy diet and regular exercise. We should love, respect, and enjoy ourselves as God does. Our physical care plan can include healthy meals at home, a workout partner, and a competent, caring physician.

Perhaps a fast is necessary for you to refocus on the Lord and flush toxins from your system. A break from solid food can help to break us from its addictive influence. Food is for our physical nourishment and emotional enjoyment, but we should not let it become an idol through over-consumption. What consumes us controls us. Perhaps you might start with a juice fast for three days before tackling a water-only fast for a week. A fast can recalibrate our physical and spiritual desires to align with God's will.

> *The Maker of our marvelous self expects us to love our body as He does.*

"When you fast, wash your face and beautify yourself with oil, so no one who looks at you will know about your discipline.

Only your Father, who is unseen, will see your fast. And your Father, who sees in secret, will reward you" (Matthew 6:17-18, The Voice).

PRAYER

Heavenly Father, my heart's desire is to nourish and care for my body as Christ does for His body, the church.

RELATED READINGS

1 SAMUEL 7:6; DANIEL 1:15-16; PSALM 139:14; MATTHEW 4:2; ACTS 14:23

NOTES

_____

_____

_____

_____

_____

_____

_____

The Holy Spirit has
such a high regard for
our bodies that He makes
His residence within us.
Our body is His temple.

Financial

WISDOM

DAY 25

Give Generously

Give away your life; you'll find life given back, but not merely given back—given back with bonus and blessing. Giving, not getting, is the way. Generosity begets generosity.

—LUKE **6:38,** MSG

*I*t is impossible to out-give the Lord, because He augments any gift given in Jesus' name with His almighty influence. He can take a penny and make it a dime. He can take a dime and make it a dollar. He can take a dollar and make it a hundred dollars. He can take a hundred dollars and make it a thousand. Eternally motivated gifts grow exponentially.

God can take one life surrendered to Jesus and influence a family. He can take a family under the Lordship of Christ and influence a church, a ministry, and a community. He can take a Christ-centered community and influence a state. He can take a state that stands for God's standards and revive a nation. Indeed, He has taken a nation founded on His principles and influenced the world. One submitted life is leverage in the Lord's hands.

"The generous will themselves be blessed, for they share their food with the poor" (Proverbs 22:9).

Would you be interested in an investment with a 100 percent guaranteed return on investment? In God's economy, gifts given for His glory are multiplied. He takes our ordinary faith offerings and converts every act of worship into extraordinary eternal results.

> *In God's economy, gifts given for His glory are multiplied.*

When you give in Jesus' name, you are giving to Jesus. The Lord is the righteous recipient of your good and generous gifts. Would your giving motivation and amount be any different if you gave to Jesus in person? Would your heart and posture bow in holy reverence and gratitude? Giving is an act of worship to holy God—not because He needs anything—but because we need to recognize our need for Him and His reward.

"Whoever is kind to the poor lends to the LORD, and he will reward them for what they have done" (Proverbs 19:17).

The Lord has chosen to meet the needs of His people through His people; He even uses unbelievers to care for believers. To those outside the faith, it is often the kindness of God through godly people that leads to repentance. Your gracious gift combined with God's grace is a conduit for people to know Christ. You cannot out-give God, but your generosity joins Him in bringing people into the saving knowledge of His Son, Jesus.

"Now he who supplies seed to the sower and bread for food will also supply and increase your store of seed and will enlarge the harvest of your righteousness. You will be enriched in every way so that you can be generous on every occasion, and through us your generosity will result in thanksgiving to God" (2 Corinthians 9:10-11).

QUESTION FOR THOUGHT AND PRAYER
Where is the Lord calling me to join Him and aggressively give in the name of Jesus?

RELATED READINGS
PSALM 146:7; MATTHEW 14:17-21; 2 CORINTHIANS 8:2; HEBREWS 6:10

NOTES

_____

_____

_____

_____

_____

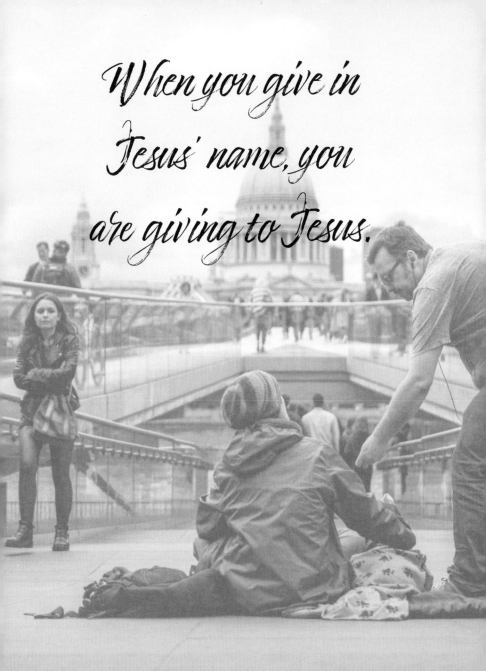

DAY 26

Save Systematically

Ants are creatures of little strength, yet they store up their food in the summer.

—Proverbs 30:25

Systematic saving is a wise way to express faith in our heavenly Father. He does His part by giving us the ability to produce resources, and He expects us not to spend it all in the present. The temptation is to take the work of our hands and have it all for now. However, when we wait on wants and save for needs, we position ourselves to give in our golden years.

"Your beginnings will seem humble, so prosperous will your future be" (Job 8:7).

Regular saving requires self-denial and self-sacrifice. This is especially hard for those who are spenders. You want to reward yourself for a job well done, so you splurge and enjoy the moment. Perhaps a good goal is to save 10 percent for long-term savings, just like you give 10 percent to the church and the Lord's work. Consider an automatic draft from your checking account into safe savings, so over time you adjust and don't miss the money.

"The wise store up choice food and olive oil, but fools gulp theirs down. Whoever pursues righteousness and love finds life, prosperity and honor" (Proverbs 21:20-21).

When you systematically save, it gives you options. Would you like to have the opportunity to take your grandchildren on mission trips or give to building orphanages around the world? Maybe. Or you may have the simple goal of having access to proper healthcare. None of us want to be a burden to family or friends.

Lead a disciplined life today and you will enjoy the fruit of fulfillment tomorrow.

"'So there is hope for your descendants,' declares the Lord. 'Your children will return to their own land'" (Jeremiah 31:17).

Wise stewards decide early on to set up a savings plan and not presume on the Lord. Use the times you gather extra income to store up for the lean times, just like Joseph saved grain during the prosperous days so he could provide during the days of famine. Your short-term sacrifice will lead to long-term security. Saving now increases giving later. Lead a disciplined life today and you will enjoy the fruit of fulfillment tomorrow.

"This food should be held in reserve for the country, to be used during the seven years of famine that will come upon Egypt, so that the country may not be ruined by the famine" (Genesis 41:36).

QUESTION FOR THOUGHT AND PRAYER
How can I save wisely for my family and my future needs?

RELATED READINGS
PROVERBS 21:5; 1 CORINTHIANS 16:2; 1 TIMOTHY 5:8

NOTES

Wise stewards decide early on to set up a savings plan and not presume on the Lord.

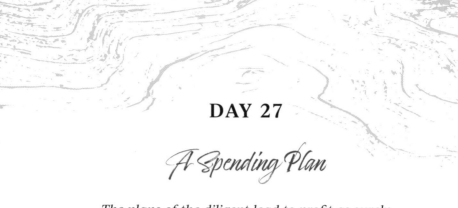

DAY 27

A Spending Plan

The plans of the diligent lead to profit as surely as haste leads to poverty.

—PROVERBS 21:5

*O*ne spouse may be frugal in spending, while the other freely spends and becomes irresponsible with expenditures. When the liberal spender becomes excessive, real repentance requires them to discuss their spending desires with their spouse before they spend money. Certainly, spending should not be hidden from your husband or wife, as this leads to loss of trust in the relationship.

What is your spending plan? For example, you may be in a financial wilderness. If so, seek the wisdom of what the Bible says about managing money. Perhaps you need to create a savings plan and, if necessary, downsize your lifestyle to lower expenses. If possible, maintain and even increase your charitable giving. Sometimes it is necessary to seek help from a seasoned financial manager, one with objective advice and strategies for your season of life.

Avoid debt. A nation, business, or home built on debt is owned and controlled by outside forces. There is no freedom or liberty to be found in financial leverage, only obligations and payment plans. Debt is unemotional and uncaring when it decides to call your loan or makes new demands you are unable to fulfill.

Implement a plan to pay down your debt. Begin by paying off the credit card with the smallest balance, and perhaps decrease your credit cards to just one and pay off the balance monthly. Eradicate your mortgage by the time your children start college and you will have added margin for their extra educational expenses. Delayed gratification is a discipline God blesses.

Turn to Christ instead of credit, and watch Him create opportunities you never conceived of. Waiting to pay in cash is an exercise in faith and a disciplining of the flesh. A smaller home and older car, with peace and contentment, is much better than the latest toys with regret and restless nights. Debt-free living liberates your life and increases your generous giving.

"Owe nothing to anyone except to love one another, for he who loves his neighbor has fulfilled the law" (Romans 13:8, NASB).

> *Delayed gratification is a discipline God blesses.*

Get-rich-quick schemes only feed greed. In God's economy, it is the one who diligently deposits smaller amounts in a secure place who reaps rewards. Wise managers make the first 10 percent of their income a gift offering in the form of a tithe to their heavenly Father and the second 10 percent an investment in their future.

Money obtained by vanity is spent on vanity, but money gained by hard work and honesty is retained for growth. Look to the Lord as your provider and see yourself as a steward of His stuff.

"Dishonest money dwindles away, but he who gathers money little by little makes it grow" (Proverbs 13:11).

QUESTION FOR THOUGHT AND PRAYER

Am I frivolously spending just for today, or am I disciplined each day to deposit a dollar toward tomorrow?

RELATED READINGS

PSALM 128:2; JEREMIAH 17:11; EPHESIANS 4:28; JAMES 5:1-5

NOTES

_____

_____

_____

_____

_____

Waiting to pay in cash is an exercise in faith and a disciplining of desires.

DAY 28

God or Money

No one can serve two masters. Either you will hate the one and love the other, or you will be devoted to the one and despise the other. You cannot serve both God and Money.

—MATTHEW 6:24

How do you know if you love God or money more? Ask yourself, do you worry more about missing your prayer time or missing your paycheck? Are you more anxious about what the Almighty thinks, or do you obsess over the opinion of others? Are you driven to seek God's Kingdom first, or to blindly build your kingdom? Devotion to the eternal or the temporal cannot be a both/and, but is a choice of which one really captures your worship.

Money makes promises it cannot keep—things like security, peace, and prosperity. But the Lord makes promises He does keep—grace, forgiveness, joy, and contentment. When the commands of these two contradict, whom will you follow: Christ or cash? Decide now, so when you are in the emotion of the moment you do not give in to glittering gold.

What keeps you up at night? Is it how to make more money or how to make more of Jesus? Set your affections above, and you will be more effective below. The Lord is looking for people with whom He can entrust more of His blessings. He longs for faithful ones who use their finances to draw lost souls to salvation, hurting people to healing, and who boldly pray, "Your Kingdom come on earth as it is in heaven."

Are you driven to seek God's Kingdom first, or to blindly build your kingdom?

You might take your family on a mission trip and see how the masses live with little money, but with a lot of the Lord. It is revolutionary for a soul that has been seduced by the mistress of money to see how believers without stuff affectionately embrace their Lord and Savior Jesus Christ. Expose your faith to the poor so you are liberated from wealth.

In the end, this is a heart issue; who captures your affections, your Savior or your stuff? Money makes a poor master, but a useful servant. On the other hand, Jesus is the trustworthy Master with whom you can place your faith and devotion. Money tries to maneuver itself into a place of priority, but by faith you can relegate it to serve righteous causes. Love Jesus, not money.

"Do not love the world or anything in the world. If anyone loves the world, love for the Father is not in them" (1 John 2:15).

QUESTION FOR THOUGHT AND PRAYER

*What masters my mind and holds my heart:
God or money? Who needs my money?*

RELATED READINGS

MALACHI 3:8-10; MATTHEW 6:10; COLOSSIANS 3:1-10; 1 TIMOTHY 6:6-10

NOTES

_____

_____

_____

_____

_____

_____

_____

_____

_____

_____

What captures your affections—your Savior or your stuff?

DAY 29

Economic Storm

When the storm has swept by, the wicked are
gone, but the righteous stand firm forever.

— **Proverbs 10:25**

*E*conomic storms expose evil, similar to the way when the ocean tide goes out, you are able to see what was hidden beneath the waves. Dead wood is swept away, no more to be seen. It may seem like the wicked are prospering, but eventually they will be found out. The Holy Spirit shakes out sin so it can be seen and judged. As the Lord promised His children in the past, "I will shake the people of Israel" (Amos 9:9).

What used to make a lot of noise and draw the attention of the elite has lost its credibility under scrutiny. Economic storms collapse businesses and ministries who are dependent on debt, and conversely they cause good churches to increase in attendance. There is a purging of pride, and all manner of excess is exposed. What really matters in life—faith, family, friends, food, and shelter—becomes the priority. Storms reveal worth.

In the midst of all this, those who cling to Christ are not shaken.

He is our cornerstone that no degree of chaos can challenge. The Bible says, "Those who trust in the Lord are like Mount Zion, which cannot be shaken but endures forever" (Psalm 125:1). The righteous cannot be moved because their Master is immovable. Therefore, stand firm in the Lord.

Furthermore, your security in your Savior Jesus is stability for you and your family, friends, and work associates. Your unwavering faith during difficult days helps them replace panic with peace, fear with faith, and compromise with conviction. Indeed, if all you have left is a firm foundation of faith, begin building back God's big vision. Are you a wise builder?

> ...those who cling to Christ are not shaken.

It takes discipline to not spend all our earnings in an instant. Commercials and our opportunities to consume exploit our emotions. Culture sucks us in and urges us to spend not all we have but more than we have, so be on guard with a simple system for savings. For example, set up an automatic draft from each paycheck that goes straight into a savings account. Preserve this cash, and one day your financial fruit tree will become an orchard.

Jesus says, "Therefore everyone who hears these words of mine and puts them into practice is like a wise man who built his house on the rock" (Matthew 7:24).

QUESTION FOR THOUGHT AND PRAYER

*How can I build my life, home,
and work on the solid rock of Jesus?*

RELATED READINGS

JOB 20:5; PSALM 37:10; ACTS 2:25; HEBREWS 12:28

NOTES

_____

_____

_____

_____

_____

_____

_____

_____

_____

_____

Your security in your
Savior Jesus is stability
for you and your family.

DAY 30

Possessions Complicate

*Their possessions were so great that they were
not able to stay together. And quarreling arose.*

—Genesis 13:6-7

*A*bram and Lot had a lot of stuff. They were blessed with
family, friends, and finances. However, things became
complicated, and they were unable to coexist with each other.
Though they needed one another, they could not stay together.

The fear of losing their possessions superseded the joy of
growing their relationship. So they divided, and as a result of
their vulnerability, Lot lost everything. Like Jesus said, "Every
city or household divided against itself will not stand"(Matthew
12:25).

Possessions are not wrong in themselves. However, when the
management of your wealth compromises your loyalty to
people, there is a problem. Possessions should be subservient
to people; otherwise things get off-kilter. People know if you
value your net worth over them. So how can you keep the right
balance between possessions and people?

Begin with an inventory of your time. How do you spend your time? Do you spend more time in managing your stuff, or loving people? You may need to sell some of your property, or better yet give it away.

Ask yourself, "Does my stuff compete with my relationship with God?" Perhaps you should downsize your stuff so you can upsize your focus on Jesus. By God's grace, use the material fortune He has entrusted to you as a magnet that draws you closer to God and people. And use your blessing of discretionary time to bless others.

"Command those who are rich in this present world not to be arrogant nor to put their hope in wealth, which is so uncertain, but to put their hope in God, who richly provides us with everything for our enjoyment. Command them to do good, to be rich in good deeds, and to be generous and willing to share. In this way they will lay up treasure for themselves as a firm foundation for the coming age, so that they may take hold of the life that is truly life" (1 Timothy 6:17-19).

Do you spend more time in managing your stuff, or loving people?

QUESTION FOR THOUGHT AND PRAYER

*How can I position my possessions so the
Lord possesses more of me and my family?*

RELATED READINGS

GENESIS 36:6-7; ECCLESIASTES 5:10-11; LUKE 3:11; 2 CORINTHIANS 9:6-15

NOTES

_____

_____

_____

_____

_____

_____

_____

_____

_____

_____

Be aware, fear of losing possessions can supersede the joy of growing relationships.

DAY 31

The Idol of Money

When he [Micah] returned the eleven hundred shekels of silver to his mother, she said, "I solemnly consecrate my silver to the LORD for my son to make an image overlaid with silver. I will give it back to you." So after he returned the silver to his mother, she took two hundred shekels of silver and gave them to a silversmith, who used them to make the idol. And it was put in Micah's house.

—JUDGES 17:3-4

What is an idol? Anything or anyone that competes for our attention, affections, and worship of Almighty God. A life loyal to the Lord has no rivals to Jesus, but a life attracted to shiny idols is easily distracted—and eventually led astray. Parents harbor idols in their home when they give a child all they want—instead of all they need. For physical safety, a loaded gun would never be entrusted to a child, yet a parent erodes their adult child's character by prematurely giving the gifts of luxury cars, big houses, and an excessive inheritance. All too soon, cash replaces Christ.

Micah (not the famous prophet) loved money more than he loved his mama or the Lord. Perhaps he feared being unable to take care of his family, so he took from his mother—most likely the inheritance she would eventually give to him. He was impatient, and so he stole her security. Upon returning his mother's money, she commissioned some of the silver to become a *graven image.* Mom only paid lip service to dedicating her dollars to God, when in reality she worshiped an idol she thought she could control. She invested her love of money into her son's heart.

"For you know that it was not with perishable things such as silver or gold that you were redeemed from the empty way of life handed down to you from your ancestors, but with the precious blood of Christ, a lamb without blemish or defect" (1 Peter 1:18-19).

A life attracted to shiny idols is easily distracted —and eventually led astray.

Money need not become an idol in your family; rather, make it an agent for good in God's hands. Let your family know that all you have is from the Lord and dedicated to the Lord—your possessions are His possessions. Practice generosity. A family who gives together will grow joyful together. Nothing keeps the idols of greed more unwelcome and uncomfortable in your home than generous giving.

Perhaps at the right time, you might set up a giving fund for each young adult child with National Christian Foundation and coach them in how to give away money. An adult child who can manage money well has a much better chance at managing life well. Most of all, keep Jesus Christ the head of your home and seek to follow Him in how to use your resources.

"Fathers, do not exasperate your children; instead, bring them up in the training and instruction of the Lord" (Ephesians 6:4).

PRAYER
Heavenly Father, all I have is Yours, multiply my assets for Your purposes in Jesus' name, amen.

RELATED READINGS
PROVERBS 13:22; EPHESIANS 5:5, 6:2; HEBREWS 12:11; 1 JOHN 3:17

NOTES

_____

_____

_____

_____

_____

Money need not become an idol in your family, rather, make it an agent for good in God's hands.

DAY 32

Rich toward God

But God said to him, "You fool! This very night your life will be demanded from you. Then who will get what you have prepared for yourself?" This is how it will be with whoever stores up things for themselves but is not rich toward God.

—LUKE 12:20-21

Am I building my barns bigger? Or am I building God's barns better? Jesus contrasts two brothers bickering over their inheritance to illustrate a heart of greed. Wealth simultaneously decreases the need for stuff and the felt need for God. If I act like I am the owner of my possessions, then the acquisition of more possessions becomes my motivation. But if I live like the Lord is the owner of my stuff and I am His steward, then the distribution of His possessions becomes my passion. Generosity starves greed.

The parable Jesus unpacks is full of emotion, wisdom, and warning. He calls out a prosperous man for his foolishness, shortsightedness, self-indulgence, and self-deception. The man thought he owned his possessions: "my crops, my barns, my grain, myself." He missed the obvious fact that the Creator of the soil, his soul, and the harvest was Almighty God. This foolish man failed to be rich toward God because he was living for himself.

"And God is able to bless you abundantly, so that in all things at all times, having all that you need, you will abound in every good work. As it is written: 'They have freely scattered their gifts to the poor; their righteousness endures forever'" (2 Corinthians 9:8-9).

Truett Cathy, the founder of Chick-fil-A, was extravagantly rich toward God. He was rich in his relationships by giving personalized encouragement, wisdom, and financial generosity. He was rich toward orphans and foster children by providing facilities and opportunities for them to feel loved and taken care of. Though he led a billion-dollar company, he lived modestly so his team members could take off from work on Sundays and take care of their families. Truett famously said about business, "If we focus on becoming better, our customers will demand we become bigger." As followers of Jesus, if we focus on becoming more like Christ, others will look to learn about following Christ. Being rich toward God is valuing what God values over ourselves.

> *Being rich toward God is valuing what God values over ourselves.*

What does it mean to be rich toward God? It means to treasure what He treasures: my relationship with Him, lost souls, and fellow believers. To be rich toward God is to be rich in good deeds, rich in generosity, and rich in relationships.

"Command those who are rich in this present world not to be arrogant nor to put their hope in wealth, which is so uncertain, but to put their hope in God, who richly provides us with everything for our enjoyment. Command them to do good, to be rich in good deeds, and to be generous and willing to share. In this way they will lay up treasure for themselves as a firm foundation for the coming age, so that they may take hold of the life that is truly life" (1 Timothy 6:17-19).

✝

PRAYER

Heavenly Father, inspire and instruct me
to be rich toward You. In Jesus' name, amen.

RELATED READINGS

1 CHRONICLES 29:14; PROVERBS 3:9, 11:25; MATTHEW 6:2; LUKE 6:30

NOTES

_____

_____

_____

_____

_____

To be rich toward God is to be rich in good deeds, rich in generosity, and rich in relationships.

DAY 33

A Compelling Call

"Come, follow me," Jesus said, "and I will send you out to fish for people." At once they left their nets and followed him.

—MATTHEW 4:19-20

Every disciple of Jesus is called by the Lord to minister wherever they are—in their home and in the marketplace. However, Christ does call some of His followers to vocational ministry. It is a calling that comes to ordinary men and women who many times accomplish extraordinary results. Whom does He call for full-time ministry? Christ's call comes to those who have a hungry heart for God.

Like Paul, you might have been suddenly smitten by a revelation of Jesus as Lord and compelled to respond. Or maybe like David you gradually went from feeding sheep what's perishable to feeding God's people the imperishable. Wherever Christ calls, His first command is to love God and His second is to love His people. A calling without love is like a car without gasoline; it may be attractive on the outside, but it's not going anywhere. Love large where the Lord has called you.

Every calling will include hardship: "You have persevered and have endured hardships for my name, and have not grown weary" (Revelation 2:3). Christians are not immune to conflict; in fact, your faith at times invites difficulty. So don't seek to shelter your life from adversity. Rather, position yourself in obedience to Christ's calling.

So don't look for your calling —look for Christ, and He will reveal His calling to you.

Make sure you minister first to your spouse and children. Don't be like the cobbler who had no shoes for his family. Your credibility for Christ comes from living your faith out with those who know you the best. What does it profit a man if he saves the whole world and loses his family? A calling to family first frees you to evangelize and disciple with God's favor.

Above all, the Lord is looking for those already engaged in His Word, growing in their character, and active in sharing their faith. It is out of your regular routine of serving Him that you will see what He has in store next. Christ's calling comes to believers who desire the Holy Spirit to conform them into the image of Christ. He calls those whom He can trust. So don't look for your calling—look for Christ, and He will reveal His calling to you.

"I, even I, have spoken; yes, I have called him. I will bring him, and he will succeed in his mission" (Isaiah 48:15).

QUESTION FOR THOUGHT AND PRAYER

What is Christ's calling for my life? Am I steadfast in loving the Lord and people?

RELATED READINGS

ACTS 9:10; 1 CORINTHIANS 7:17; HEBREWS 5:4; REVELATION 7:14

NOTES

_____

_____

_____

_____

_____

_____

_____

Every disciple of Jesus is called by the Lord to minister wherever they are — in their home and in the marketplace. However, Christ does call some of His followers to vocational ministry.

DAY 34

Be Respectable

Now the overseer is to be above reproach, faithful to his wife, temperate, self-controlled, respectable, hospitable, able to teach, not given to drunkenness, not violent but gentle, not quarrelsome, not a lover of money.

—1 TIMOTHY 3:2-3

*R*espectability invites respect. If you're complaining, "I can't get any respect," are you trying to get respect based on your charm, charisma, or ability to converse well? These qualities do not mean you are respectable; in fact, they can repel respect and garner disrespect. Your skills and gifts require character to attain the admiration of others.

Respect is earned, not demanded. It is sustained by influence, not position. Presidents, preachers, and parents are given respect by their position, but if they consistently underperform or lack integrity, they lose respect. It is not a right of the irresponsible, but a privilege of the dependable. Respectable leaders get right results in the right way.

"Choose some wise, understanding and respected men from each of your tribes, and I will set them over you" (Deuteronomy 1:13).

Respectable leaders also rise to the occasion and do the right things. They persevere and provide stability, instead of panicking and creating chaos. They take responsibility by espousing the values of the organization, not by gossiping and blaming others. There is a depth of character that runs deep within their soul, not to be stolen by sin.

A respectable leader is highly prized when their track record is one of trustworthiness, honesty, and follow-through. However, the goal is not for people to like you. They may not like you when you lovingly hold them accountable, but they will respect you. They may not like your discipline, but they will respect your consistency.

Respectability invites respect.

They may not embrace your beliefs, but if expressed in humility, they will respect you. The question to ask is, "Am I respectable?" If so, you can expect respect.

"Teach the older men to be temperate, worthy of respect, self-controlled, and sound in faith, in love and in endurance" (Titus 2:2).

"A sensible person wins admiration, but a warped mind is despised" (Proverbs 12:8, NLT).

QUESTION FOR THOUGHT AND PRAYER
*What area of my character needs growth
and transformation in order to solicit respect?*

RELATED READINGS
EXODUS 18:21; PROVERBS 15:27; JOHN 10:12-13; ROMANS 16:18

NOTES

Respect is earned over time, not demanded in an instant.

DAY 35

Execute with Excellence

Those who work their land will have abundant food, but those who chase fantasies have no sense.

—Proverbs 12:11

outine work may not be sexy, but it is necessary. We must meet our needs and the needs of those who depend on us. The same work—day in and day out—can seem simple and even boring, but it is a test of our faithfulness. Will I continue to faithfully carry out uncomplicated responsibilities, even when my attention span dwindles? This kind of faithfulness is God's path to blessing. "Steady plodding brings prosperity" (Proverbs 21:5, TLB).

The contrast to routine work is chasing after get-rich-quick schemes that make promises they can't keep. Be careful not to be led astray by fantasies that lead nowhere. It is false faith to think a gimmick or some conniving circumstance can replace hard work. Wisdom stops chasing after the next scheme and sticks instead to the certainty of available work. What does your spouse say is the smart thing to do? Give them all the facts and listen to their response to gain wisdom.

"They sow the wind and reap the whirlwind. The stalk has no head; it will produce no flour" (Hosea 8:7).

Work can seem easy when everything is going well—when there is no evidence of a pending job loss or an increase in responsibilities with less pay. However, it is during stressful times that Christ followers can step up and set the example. Your attitude of hope and hard work is a testimony of trust in the Lord.

So stay engaged in completing your tasks with excellence even when it's hard, and you will inspire others to their labor of love. Your routine work can be an act of worship of the Lord if done with that attitude. He will bless your faithfulness to follow through with the smallest of details. Routine work with the right attitude reaps a rich reward. Are you content to serve Christ in your current career?

Routine work with the right attitude reaps a rich reward.

"Whatever you do, work at it with all your heart, as working for the Lord, not for human masters, since you know that you will receive an inheritance from the Lord as a reward. It is the Lord Christ you are serving" (Colossians 3:23-24).

QUESTION FOR THOUGHT AND PRAYER

*Is my routine work a compelling testimony
to the excellence of God's gracious work?*

RELATED READINGS

GENESIS 2:15; 1 KINGS 19:19; ROMANS 12:11; 1 TIMOTHY 4:11-12

NOTES

Excellent work gives us credibility to share our faith in God and love for Him.

DAY 36

Travel Temptations

My husband is not at home; he has gone on a long journey. He took his purse filled with money and will not be home till full moon.

—Proverbs 7:19-20

How do you deal with temptations when you travel? Conversely, what is your behavior when you are the spouse left back at home? Is your house a palace of peace, or a prison of confinement? It is not only the weary traveler who needs to be wary of wrong behavior; the one left "holding down the fort" at home must be careful as well.

As a couple, you should craft together guidelines defining what you will and will not do while separated by travel. Distance can grow the heart fonder and more faithful, or it can fan the flames of lust and infidelity.

If you travel for your work, you most likely are motivated to meet the needs of your family. However, every assignment is for a season, so maybe it's time to get off the road and reconnect with your child who is approaching their teenage years, or to be there more often for your spouse who is starved for extra emotional support. Be willing to adjust with the seasons of life.

Do not drift into travel temptations that become divisive and deteriorate your marriage. One boundary may be to avoid bars and go back to your room soon after work and dinner. Make it a priority when at all possible to travel with another person of similar values. A righteous routine on the road gets the right results. Be bold by becoming an influencer of integrity: good, clean fun without flirting with sin.

> *Travel temptations are terminated on both ends through trust in the Lord and trust in each other.*

On the other hand, your role in the marriage may be to daily support the children and manage the home. Take pride rather than self-pity in this season of unselfish service. By God's grace, you are molding your children's minds to the things of Christ and teaching them to influence the culture with His Kingdom priorities.

The one who stays home is as valuable as the one out working to provide for the family. Both are working to preserve the family. Stay occupied in prayer, Bible study, the children's lives, and being available for those who need you. Marriage is a team effort that sees outstanding outcomes when you are both on the same page of love and obedience to Christ. Travel temptations are terminated on both ends through trust in the Lord and trust in each other.

"'He trusts in the Lord,' they say, 'let the Lord rescue him. Let him deliver him, since he delights in him'" (Psalm 22:8).

QUESTION FOR THOUGHT AND PRAYER
What behavior boundaries do I need to create with my spouse related to our time apart?

RELATED READINGS
NUMBERS 5:11-15; LUKE 12:39-46; 1 JOHN 3:9

NOTES

A righteous routine on the road gets the right results.

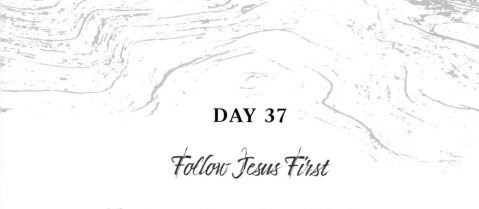

DAY 37

Follow Jesus First

> *When Jesus saw the crowd around him, he gave orders to cross to the other side of the lake. Then a teacher of the law came to him and said, "Teacher, I will follow you wherever you go."*
>
> — **MATTHEW 8:18-19**

Good leaders are first good followers. Do you follow the orders of Jesus? When He asks you to do the uncomfortable, do you move out of your comfort zone with confidence? Compelling Christian leadership requires focused followership of the Master, the Lord Jesus. Where is He asking you to go that requires sacrifice and unconditional commitment? His orders do not always make sense, but they are totally trustworthy and helpful.

When the Lord directs you to leave the noise of the crowds to the quietness of a few, do not delay. If you are obsessed by activity, you can easily lose your edge on energy and faith. When all your oomph is consumed by serving every request and answering every call, you have no time or concentration to hear from Christ. What is He saying? This is the most important inquiry you can make. What is Jesus telling you to do? When you listen, you learn.

You may be in the middle of a monster season of success. If so, make sure your achievements do not muffle the Lord's message. It is when we are going fast and

> *Follow Jesus first, and go wherever He goes.*

furious that our faith becomes perfunctory and predictable. Leadership requires alone time to retool and recalibrate our character. People follow when they know you've been with Jesus.

The most difficult part of all this may be the transition from doing less, to listening and thinking more. If you as the leader are not planning ahead, who is? Who has the best interest of the enterprise in mind? Who is defending the mission and vision of the organization so there is not a drift into competing strategies? Follow Jesus first; He will free you to see.

Where is the Lord leading you to go? Will you lag behind with excellent excuses, or will you make haste and move forward by faith? Go with God, and He will direct you through the storms of change. He may seem silent at times, but remember that He led you to this place, and where He leads, He provides. Follow Jesus first, and go wherever He goes. You may lose some people in the process, but you will gain better people for His next phase.

"Then Jesus said to his disciples, 'Whoever wants to be my disciple must deny themselves and take up their cross and follow me'" (Matthew 16:24).

QUESTION FOR THOUGHT AND PRAYER

*Where is Jesus leading me to go? Am I willing
to let go and trust Him with what's next?*

RELATED READINGS

NUMBERS 32:11; ISAIAH 8:10-12; 1 CORINTHIANS 1:11-13; REVELATION 14:4

NOTES

_____

_____

_____

_____

_____

_____

_____

_____

_____

_____

The best leaders
are first good
followers of Jesus.

DAY 38

Enjoy Your Work

> *So I saw that there is nothing better for men*
> *than that they should be happy in their work,*
> *for that is what they are here for, and no one*
> *can bring them back to life to enjoy what will be*
> *in the future, so let them enjoy it now.*
>
> — Ecclesiastes 3:22, TLB

Do you enjoy your work? Do you *really* enjoy your work? There have been seasons in my career when work was not fun. In fact, it was drudgery. My health was affected, my emotional state was fragile, and my mental condition was foggy. Going to work was like looking forward to a root canal or a firing squad. Thankless, boring, not challenging—a dead-end road. When I was younger, I had more energy than sense, so I just worked harder. But now, a few years down the road, I look for a better way. Now I pray, "Lord, how can my work be fulfilling for You?"

God made us to work. Labor is our blessing to enjoy and our burden to bear. There is nothing more fulfilling than to feel the Lord's pleasure in our job and nothing more distressing than to feel fear and frustration in just grinding out a living.

Solomon, the writer of Ecclesiastes, was either in a midlife crisis striving to learn contentment, or he was moving on to something more significant in his career. He knew firsthand the wisdom of enjoying work now and not being deceived into thinking that somewhere in the future, wealth would bring happiness. Enjoy your work now.

"A person can do nothing better than to eat and drink and find satisfaction in their own toil. This too, I see, is from the hand of God, for without him, who can eat or find enjoyment?" (Ecclesiastes 2:24-25).

Is your labor led by your love for the Lord or by your love of a competing idol? Without God's will in the middle of your motivation to make money, money will become a distrustful tyrant over your faith, family, and work. Maybe Christ has you in a place of service and influence to convert the work culture towards your values of: selflessness, wisdom (what is the wise thing to do?), and growth. If cultural change is not an option now, the Spirit may lead you to serve in another company where your values better align with the culture. Either way, enjoy your work now.

> *Is your labor led by your love for the Lord or by your love of a competing idol?*

It may be an appropriate time to get away from work, to be still and quiet before the Lord. Ask for His vocational vision for your life. Don't settle for a paycheck to just pay bills and feed your family (though this is admirable). Acknowledge seasons of testing and trials in your toil, but know that you can enjoy your work even when it's hard. Consider how you can use your expertise and experience to best love people and honor God where you are right now. Fulfilling work is Christ's best for you.

"In vain you rise early and stay up late, toiling for food to eat—for he grants sleep to those he loves" (Psalm 127:2).

QUESTION FOR THOUGHT AND PRAYER

Am I enjoying God's best in my career, or do I need to consider other options? How can my work bring joy to others?

RELATED READINGS

GENESIS 3:17; PROVERBS 31:31; JOHN 4:34, 17:4; 1 TIMOTHY 5:18

NOTES

_____

_____

_____

_____

_____

Acknowledge seasons of testing and trials in your toil, but know that you can enjoy your work even when it's hard.

DAY 39

Fulfilling Work

*When his master saw that the L*ORD *was with him and that the L*ORD *gave him success in everything he did, Joseph found favor in his eyes and became his attendant. Potiphar put him in charge of his household, and he entrusted to his care everything he owned.*

—GENESIS 39:3-4

What brings you fulfillment in your work? Is it the sense of accomplishment at a completed task? Is it the opportunity to encourage someone? Is it the satisfaction of caring for your family? Is it the sense of security from a steady income stream? Your vocational fulfillment likely flows from a combination of these characteristics and more. When you are fulfilled in your job, you are able to filter through the negatives on the way to the positives. "Many people mistake our work for our vocation. Our vocation is the love of Jesus."[1]

Be careful not to equate feeling passionate about your position with being fulfilled in your work. Passions ebb and flow around the excitement of a situation. In a start-up, everyone is thinking and working twenty-four hours a day, seven days a week. But this passionate, breakneck pace is not sustainable. Your career is a marathon, not a sprint. On the other hand, if down the road you are still happy and absorbed in your work, not constantly glancing at the clock, then it is likely you are in a place of fulfillment.

"He named him Noah and said, 'He will comfort us in the labor and painful toil of our hands caused by the ground the Lord has cursed'" (Genesis 5:29). Is it your sense of control over the outcome that draws you to serve where you work? You feel empowered, you are able to expand your skills, and you can make a meaningful contribution in your community as a parent or an employee. Vocational fulfillment flows from a heart engaged in a mission that means something to you and to the Lord.

God blesses the work He assigns. Have you accepted the Lord's assignment?

Christ has placed you where you are; can you be content to serve Him wholeheartedly? The Almighty's vocational assignment carries its own sense of satisfaction. Joseph found favor because God placed him in his leadership role. In the same way, use your workplace platform as a launching pad for the Lord. Your ability to support others, offer promotions, and create a caring culture facilitates fulfillment for those around you. Vocational fulfillment is a faith journey that brings out the best in you and those you serve. God blesses the work He assigns. Have you accepted the Lord's assignment?

"From the time he put him in charge of his household and of all that he owned, the Lord blessed the household of the Egyptian because of Joseph" (Genesis 39:5).

PRAYER

Heavenly Father, lead me to Your work, and help me not to be distracted by other good work. In Jesus' name, amen.

RELATED READINGS

DEUTERONOMY 15:10; PSALM 90:17;
PROVERBS 12:11; COLOSSIANS 3:24; 1 TIMOTHY 5:8

NOTES

_____

_____

_____

_____

_____

_____

_____

Many people mistake
our work for our
vocation. Our vocation
is the love of Jesus.[1]

— MOTHER TERESA

[1] Mother Teresa, see https://www.azquotes.com/quote/292151.

DAY 40

Working for the Lord

Whatever you do, work at it with all your heart, as working for the Lord, not for human masters, since you know that you will receive an inheritance from the Lord as a reward. It is the Lord Christ you are serving.

—Colossians 3:23-24

She worked tirelessly as she meticulously cleaned the hospital room. Every object shone brightly after her sanitized rag rubbed over the surface of the metal mirror frame, the elaborate bed support, the mobile meal table—all surfaces harboring germs. My wife, Rita, recognizing the hospital attendant's energetic work, commented, "Teresa, you must sleep well at night." She replied, "I sleep well every night. The Lord gives me good sleep. I work for the Lord. I used to do those drugs and alcohol, but not for seven years. I was rescued, and now I work for the Lord."

Teresa continued, "I worked my way up to this job (custodian), and I am glad I can do good work for all these people who need me. Like your mother (Rita's mom was very ill). She's going to be ok. She is a good woman. Reminds me of my momma. My momma saw me work here for three years before she passed.

Yes, momma saw me work for the Lord and not do those old drugs and alcohol." Rita felt she was in the presence of greatness—a great woman who acknowledged and served her great God. Teresa's gratitude was infectious, and her work ethic for her Lord was worshipful!

"Do not work for food that spoils, but for food that endures to eternal life, which the Son of Man will give you. For on him God the Father has placed his seal of approval" (John 6:27).

What is the motivation behind your work? A paycheck to put food on the table, furniture in the house, gas in the car, children in school, and eventually retirement? If this is your small, self-focused perspective, there is a much larger and more fulfilling vision to embrace. The Lord Jesus Christ is the owner of all commerce and economic development. God is in charge of job placement, promotions, and career advancement. The Holy Spirit moves the hearts of decision makers to make the choices that align with the Lord's will. So work for the Lord's eternal ways.

> *Boldly declare that you work for the Lord! He gives you purpose, and He gives you peace.*

Never get over your gratitude to God for the physical, mental, emotional, and spiritual health to carry out your job responsibilities. Manage yourself and your time as if your Master Jesus might drop by at any time and inspect your work. What would He find? Diligence or half-heartedness? Excellence or expedience? Counting the minutes or wondering where the time went? Take whatever means necessary so your work means something. Boldly declare that you work for the Lord! He gives you purpose, and He gives you peace.

"Why spend money on what is not bread, and your labor on what does not satisfy? Listen, listen to me, and eat what is good, and you will delight in the richest of fare" (Isaiah 55:2).

PRAYER

Heavenly Father, help me not forget that I work for You and with You to do great work.

RELATED READINGS

ECCLESIASTES 6:2; ISAIAH 49:4; HOSEA 4:10-11;
HAGGAI 1:6; MATTHEW 16:27

NOTES

Manage yourself
and your time as
if your Master
Jesus might drop
by at any time and
inspect your work.

How to Become

A DISCIPLE OF JESUS CHRIST

My process for finding God covered a span of nineteen years, before I truly understood my need for His love and forgiveness in a personal relationship with Jesus Christ. Along this path of spiritual awakening, many people in my life contributed to my progress in knowing God. My mother took me to church at age twelve so I could learn about faith through the confirmation process. My grandmother modeled her walk with Jesus by being kind and generous to everyone she encountered. In college, I begin attending church with Rita (my future wife) and her family.

Weekly relevant teaching from an ancient book—the Bible—began to answer many of life's questions. I was intrigued by questions like, What is God's plan for my life? Who is Jesus Christ? What is sin, salvation, heaven, and hell? How can I live an abundant life of forgiveness, joy, and love?

The Lord found me first with His incredible love, and then when I surrendered in repentance and faith in Jesus, I found Him. For two years, a businessman in our church showed me how to grow in grace through Bible study, prayer, sharing my faith, and service to others. Each day I still discover more of God's great love and His new mercies.

Are you intrigued like I was? Here is an outline for finding God and becoming a disciple of Jesus:

BELIEVE

"If you declare with your mouth, 'Jesus is Lord,' and believe in your heart that God raised him from the dead, you will be saved" (Romans 10:9). Belief in Jesus Christ as your Savior and Lord gives you eternal life in heaven.

REPENT AND BE BAPTIZED

"Peter replied, 'Repent and be baptized, every one of you, in the name of Jesus Christ for the forgiveness of your sins. And you will receive the gift of the Holy Spirit'" (Acts 2:38). Repentance means turning from your sin and publicly confessing Christ in baptism.

OBEY

"Jesus replied, 'Anyone who loves me will obey my teaching. My Father will love them, and we will come to them and make our home with them'" (John 14:23).

WORSHIP, PRAYER, COMMUNITY, EVANGELISM, AND STUDY

"Every day they continued to meet together in the temple courts. They broke bread in their homes and ate together with glad and sincere hearts, praising God and enjoying the favor of all the people. And the Lord added to their number daily those who were being saved" (Acts 2:46-47).

LOVE GOD

"Jesus replied: "'Love the Lord your God with all your heart and with all your soul and with all your mind.' This is the first and greatest commandment'" (Matthew 22:37-38).

LOVE PEOPLE

"And the second is like it: 'Love your neighbor as yourself'" (Matthew 22:39).

MAKE DISCIPLES

"And the things you have heard me say in the presence of many witnesses entrust to reliable people who will also be qualified to teach others" (2 Timothy 2:2).

What Others Are Saying about Wisdom Hunters

#1 – *I LOVE your daily devotions. Each day I am hearing just what I need to hear, and every day I am finding someone to share that day's devotion with who also needs that lesson at that time. Thank you so much! Truly, thank you! Sue*

#2 – *I find your devotionals to be truthful and uplifting to the spirit. Because I am so encouraged by the Holy Spirit using you, through His Word I share very often to strengthen my brothers and sisters as I am strengthened. On July 31st "You Matter" ministered so to my heart. My soul and spirit were washed with tears as the Word validated me. Thanks! Lois*

#3 – *Thank you for sharing His wisdom each day. Your devotionals are always insightful, and I look forward to reading them each morning. As I go about my day I think about their truth and they encourage me to be more like Him. Blessings! Cindy*

#4 – *Thank you for affirming my tears of joy this morning. Heard a message about adoptive parents' struggles and not giving up. I identified with it as I am an adoptive parent that never gave up and we feel only joy after all of the pain.*

#5 – *When we ask for wisdom, I think we expect an immediate infusion of knowledge and superior thinking. But for me your last two posts reminded me that I need to accept instruction and listen respectfully and carefully to the other person. Then God can impart wisdom because I am honoring and obeying Him and*

am prepared to accept it. Whatever God gives us is for His Glory through our obedience.

#6 – Good Word. It wounds then it heals beautifully.

#7 – Appointments with God–words cannot express how I felt reading this devotional. It brought tears to my eyes and was just what I needed to jump start my day. It is so easy to get caught up with time, we think we don't have enough, being pulled in every direction by everyone. Just as I ask for "me time" from my family, God is asking for the same, and how can I NOT give it to Him? Thank you, Lord, for never cancelling Your appointments. I will read this daily to keep me in spiritual-check. Be Blessed! Peggy

#8 – How many times I have lost all hope and was touched by the daily devotions. My daughter died several years ago, then my husband died of cancer. My son remarried and they have kept my dear sweet grandchildren from me. I have lost my whole family, but I know that the Lord will never leave me nor forsake me. He is the rock upon I stand. So many times your devotions are just what I needed for the day. Thank you! Gail

#9 – I have learned so much even though I learned at a late age. With God it's never too late, and I feel so special that God and Jesus loves me enough to include me in His Kingdom of heaven. God sent you, Mr. Boyd Bailey. I pray many others who think that their lives are not worth living, as I did, would be reached by godly, wise people such as you! Chong

WISDOM HUNTER RESOURCES by BOYD BAILEY
http://www.wisdomhunters.com/bookstore_category/books/

A Guide to Lectio Divina
SACRED READING

Choose a word or phrase of the Scriptures you wish to pray. It makes no difference which text is chosen, as long as you have no set goal of "covering" a certain amount of text. The amount of text covered is in the Holy Spirit's hands, not yours.

- Read -

Turn to the text and read it slowly, gently. Savor each portion of the reading, constantly listening to the "still, small voice" of a word or phrase that somehow says, "I love you today." Do not expect lightning and ecstasies. God is teaching us to listen, to seek Him in silence. Our heavenly Father does not reach out and grab us but gently invites us ever more deeply into His presence. Silence is the language of God, so become fluent in silence.

- Ponder -

Take the word or phrase into your heart. Memorize it and slowly repeat it, allowing Scripture to interact with your inner world of concerns, memories, and ideas. Do not be afraid of distractions. Memories or thoughts are simply parts of yourself that, when they rise up, are asking to be given to God along with the rest of your being. Allow this inner pondering, this rumination, to invite you into dialogue with the Lord.

- Pray -

Whether you use words, ideas, or images — or all three — is not important. Interact with God as you would with one who you know loves and accepts you. Trust Christ with what you have discovered during your experience of meditation.

The goal of *lectio divina* is to be in the presence of God by praying the Scriptures.

Adapted from Fr. Luke Dysinger, a Benedictine
monk of Saint Andrew's Abbey, Valyermo, CA

WISDOM HUNTERS

Applying Unchanging Truth in a Changing World

Discover the inspiration and resources needed to encourage wise living and decision making in your everyday life. Join us on this wisdom journey by experiencing our diversity of environments:

Wisdom Hunters App

With convenient access and intuitive design, enjoy all of our past and present resources in one place. Available for Apple and Android.

Wisdom Hunters Podcast

A twice-a-month lively interaction with our team and guests discussing the behind-the-scenes of our most popular devotions. Available on our app, website or iTunes.

wisdomhunters.com

WISDOM HUNTERS

Wisdom Hunters Audio Devotional

A recording of our daily devotions found exclusively on our app. Ideal for travel or a quiet moment at home or work to be spiritually refreshed.

Wisdom Hunters Email

Our long-term and most popular way to receive our daily devotional content, with the choice of a daily devotional or a weekly summary sent on Saturdays. Subscribe at wisdomhunters.com and receive a free devotional book.

Wisdom Hunters Social Media

Facebook, Instagram, Twitter, and Pinterest are all places to access real time and rich devotional content.

WISDOM for *Living*

ABOUT THE AUTHOR

*B*oyd Bailey is the president of the National Christian Foundation in Georgia. His passion is to love leaders and help them grow in their journey of generosity with Jesus.

Since 2004, he has also served as president and founder of Wisdom Hunters, a ministry that connects people to Christ through devotional writings, with more than 150,000 daily followers by email, social media, podcast, and the Wisdom Hunters app.

In 1999, Boyd cofounded Ministry Ventures, which has trained leaders in approximately 1,000 faith-based nonprofits, and coached for certification more than 200 ministries in the best practices of prayer, board development, ministry model, administration, and fund-raising. By God's grace, these ministries have raised more than $100 million, and thousands of people have been led into growing relationships with Jesus Christ.

Prior to Ministry Ventures, Boyd was the national director for Crown Financial Ministries. He was instrumental in the expansion of Crown into 30 major markets across the United States. He was a key facilitator in the $25 million merger between Christian Financial Concepts and Crown Financial Ministries.

Before his work with Crown, Boyd, with Andy Stanley, started First Baptist of Atlanta's north campus. As an elder, Boyd also assisted Andy in the start of North Point Community Church.

Boyd received a Bachelor of Arts from Jacksonville State University and a Master of Divinity from Southwestern Seminary in Fort Worth, Texas. Boyd and his wife, Rita, live in Roswell, Georgia. They have been married 38 years and are blessed with four daughters, four sons-in-law, and seven grandchildren.

WISDOM HUNTERS

*H*e who walks with wise men will be wise, but the companion of fools will suffer harm" (Proverbs 13:20 NASB).

In 2003, Boyd Bailey began to informally email personal reflections from his morning devotional time to a select group of fellow wisdom hunters. Over time, these informal emails grew into Wisdom Hunters Daily Devotional. Today, thanks to God's favor and faithful followers, these emails and social media posts reach more than 150,000 readers each day.

Boyd remains relentless in the pursuit of wisdom and continues to daily write raw, original, real-time reflections from his personal encounters with the Lord.

Visit www.WisdomHunters.com where you can:

- Subscribe to free daily devotional emails
- Find out how to access our blog, Facebook, Twitter, Instagram, and the new Wisdom Hunters podcast
- Choose from a wide selection of devotional books on marriage, wisdom, wise living, and money; with books also for graduates, fathers, mothers, and more (eBook and print versions available)
- Download the free Wisdom Hunters app for Apple and Android

The thoughtful comments and wisdom our followers share each day can help us all in our journey with God.

National Christian
FOUNDATION®

*F*ounded in 1982 and based in Atlanta, Georgia, the National Christian Foundation (NCF) is a charitable giving ministry that provides wise giving solutions, mobilizes resources, and inspires biblical generosity for Christian families, advisors, and charities. NCF is currently the ninth-largest US nonprofit, having accepted more than $9 billion in contributions. It has granted more than $7 billion to more than 40,000 charities. The NCF Giving Fund, or donor-advised fund, allows donors to make charitable contributions and then recommend grants to the charities they care about, over time. NCF is also an industry leader in accepting gifts of appreciated assets, such as stocks, real estate, and business interests, which enables donors to save on taxes and align their charitable goals with their family, business, estate, and legacy plans. Learn more about NCF at www. NCFgiving.com.

MORE GREAT HARVEST HOUSE BOOKS
BY BOYD BAILEY

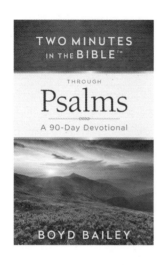

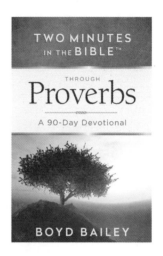

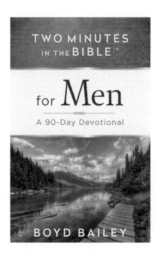

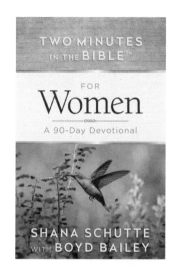

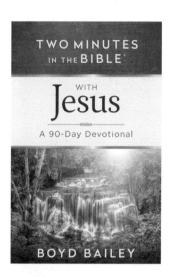

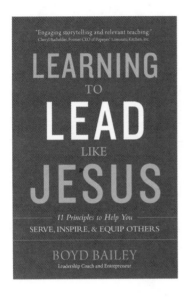

Learning to Lead Like Jesus

It's incredible when someone uses their gifts to make you feel valued and inspire you to greatness. What does it take to develop that kind of heart and influence? How can you become a leader like Jesus?

Join Boyd Bailey as he shows you how to mirror Jesus's heart and make a positive difference in those around you. Explore 11 common traits that mark successful leaders, and learn the keys to growth in wisdom and humility. Through practical teaching, you will find that great leadership begins when you turn your focus to God and model Him in your attitude, conversations, and actions.

A faithful life and humble spirit make you a leader worth following. When you lean into the Lord and learn from His example of perfect leadership, you will see lives transformed—beginning with your own!

NOTES

NOTES

NOTES

NOTES